THE PORTMANTEAU BOOK

Books by Thomas Rockwell

Rackety Bang

Squawwwk!

The Neon Motorcycle

How to Eat Fried Worms

The Portmanteau Book

THE PORTMANTEAU BOOK

by

Thomas Rockwell

Illustrated by
Gail Rockwell

LITTLE, BROWN AND COMPANY
BOSTON   TORONTO

COPYRIGHT © 1974 BY THOMAS ROCKWELL

ALL RIGHTS RESERVED. NO PART OF THIS BOOK MAY BE REPRODUCED IN ANY FORM OR BY ANY ELECTRONIC OR MECHANICAL MEANS INCLUDING INFORMATION STORAGE AND RETRIEVAL SYSTEMS WITHOUT PERMISSION IN WRITING FROM THE PUBLISHER, EXCEPT BY A REVIEWER WHO MAY QUOTE BRIEF PASSAGES IN A REVIEW.

FIRST EDITION

T 09/74

```
Library of Congress Cataloging in Publication Data

Rockwell, Thomas, 1933-
    The portmanteau book.

    SUMMARY: Stories, poems, and nonsense for all
moods and conditions.
    1. Wit and humor, Juvenile. [1. Wit and humor]
I. Rockwell, Gail, illus. II. Title.
PN6162.R62         818'.5'407         73-13588
ISBN 0-316-75341-6
ISBN 0-316-75342-4 (pbk.)
```

Published simultaneously in Canada
by Little, Brown & Company (Canada) Limited

PRINTED IN THE UNITED STATES OF AMERICA

CONTENTS

Foreword	7
An Ode by a Boy with Eight Sisters	9
HOT I: NAKEDNESS	10
The Crocodile *A Story*	16
AGNES MacPHERSON *A Daydream*	17
THE GREAT DUCK RESCUE *An Eyewitness Report*	20
CRAZY TOM	29
SIX BONUS PAGES *A Comic Book*	31
THE VAMP	37
HOT II: *toiletpaper*	38
MYSTERY PAGE	47
TWO BONUS PAGES *A Star-Spangled Contest*	48
STILTON CHEESE AND SILENCE *and Other Poems . . .*	50
HOT III: UNDERWEAR	60
JAAAAAACK MEARS! A CAUTIONARY TALE	78
FRIED HALL CLOSET *A Children's Cookbook*	85
:BACKWARDS: *Yrots A*	93
BIG BONUS GAME SECTION	99
LOONY BIN	107

Breaking Loose An Epic *(though of modest proportions)*	112
SEVEN BONUS PAGES	11,004
HOT IV: LOVE	124
Consolation Page	129
Answers to Big Bonus Game Section	129
INDEX	130
RESULTS OF A POLL	135

portmanteau: *noun* — a traveling bag; *esp.* a large gladstone bag; *adj.* — combining more than one quality.

THE PORTMANTEAU BOOK is a traveling book, a book for all seasons and weathers, all moods and conditions. A book to carry about on trains, to the beach, down Mill Street to Sally Hawkins's house. A book for a cozy night by the fire when the wind rattles the shutters and dead leaves rustle under the porch steps. A book to prop on your stomach and browse through on a hot, still August afternoon in a gently swaying hammock. A book for the school bus jouncing and rumbling home through a warm, rainy afternoon in April. A book to console yourself with, guilty and supperless on your bed in the twilight, your family's talk floating faintly up the stairs from the dining room . . .

Because THE PORTMANTEAU BOOK contains not just sad stories or funny poems or recipes for onion soup, not just philanthropy or literature or morals or plumbing. THE PORTMANTEAU BOOK contains:

6½ stories
  (one is divided into four parts):
    I: Nakedness
    II: Toiletpaper
    III: Underwear
    IV: Love

a loony bin

a cookbook

an epic
  (though of modest proportions)

an eyewitness account of *The Great Duck Rescue*

a poll

a cautionary tale
   (in which a boy forgets January, February, March, April, May, and twenty-one days in June and so doesn't go to school on Monday morning)

poems of food and passion
   and machinery

Sdrawkcab
a MYSTERY PAGE

four bonus pages
   (including an exciting contest and a complete Comic Book — 'Sergeant Buck Slasher and the Dirty Bunch')

an index containing a bank robbery

And there are no words to look up in THE PORTMANTEAU BOOK. If you come on a word you don't know, please write to the publisher, enclosing a list of the words you do know, and we will pick one from your list and send it back to you so that you may substitute it for the mysterious stranger.

Satisfaction is guaranteed. (If dissatisfied for any reason, return this book to the publishers with $12.95 in cash or money order — to cover postage and bureaucracy — and your purchase price will be cheerfully refunded.)

Recommended for all ages
but 9–12, 4–5, 12–14, 6–8,
2–3, 14–up, 1–down.

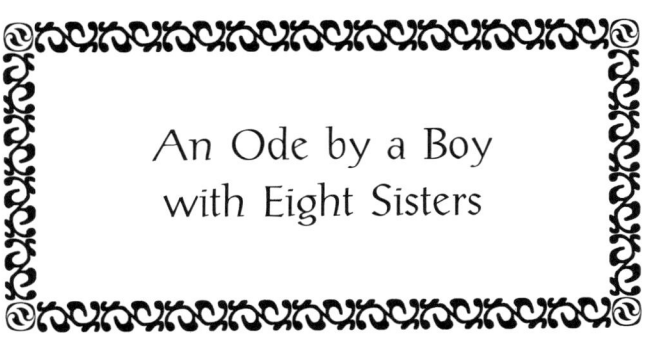

An Ode by a Boy with Eight Sisters

Glop and manure
I wish I had fewer.

HOT 1: NAKEDNESS

It was as hot as the inside of a rattlesnake. When you raised your head to look up the street, the telephone poles wobbled and shimmered in a red haze; the empty chairs outside the fire station swam on the concrete.

In the shade of his pith helmet Tim's face was red and sweating. He lagged behind me and Steve, scuffing his feet and complaining.

"Shut up," I said. "We're almost there."

"Suppose he don't let us in?"

"Why wouldn't he let us in? We're customers. It's a public drugstore."

"Yeah, but suppose he asks us how much we got to spend?" said Steve.

"Yeah," panted Tim. "Suppose that?"

"So we got twenty-five cents."

"Yeah, but you're supposed to spend fifteen cents each."

"He never asks unless it's crowded."

We pushed into Manson's Drugstore.

"Geez," said Steve, taking off his straw cowboy hat and wiping his forehead, "feel that lovely air conditioner."

We stood by the door in the cool blast, waiting for our eyes to grow accustomed to the dimness. Faceless kids sprawled in the booths along the wall, on the stools at the soda fountain. Behind the counter Mary Srodulski was drying a glass, her white jacket stained with chocolate ice cream and catsup.

"There's Albert," said Steve.

"Where?"

"In the corner. I recognize his sneakers."

"Them're *Joe's.* Nobody wears two left sneakers but Joe."

"Naw, he's got his foot twisted, he's lying on his back in the booth."

"Maybe so."

We went over. I kicked the table leg. Albert opened one eye and then closed it. Joe was opposite, his head and arms sprawled on the table. He turned his head to gaze dully at us.

"Rise and shine," said Steve. Albert groaned and sat up to make room for me. Steve slid in beside Joe. I sent Tim for two dime Cokes. He's my little brother, so when he comes along, he has to run errands.

"What're you doing?" I said.

"Yawgh," groaned Albert.

"Geez, it's hot out," said Steve.

Nobody said anything. Tim came back with the Cokes, sat down beside me and Albert, blew the paper off a straw and began to drink one of the Cokes under the shade of his pith helmet.

"Save me some," I said.

Ssssssssssssss. Mary Srodulski was making someone a soda. The phone rang in the back room. Mr. Manson began to argue with someone about a prescription.

"Geez, it's *hot*," I said.

The phone banged down and Mr. Manson came out of the back and began to argue with Mary about something. A lady came in and asked for a bottle of permanganate of slapdash. The fiery street glared in at us as the door sighed shut behind her.

"It's so hot," said Albert with his eyes closed, "that Harold Tucker's mother said he didn't have to wear his snap-on bow tie today or even button his shirt collar. I seen him hiding behind the lilac bush at the side of his house."

"Geez," I said, "how could he bring himself to come out *naked* like that?"

"Yeah, it's not like he was Tim here," Steve grinned. "*He* does it every other week."

From under the pith helmet: "I do not."

"How about last Wednesday?"

"That was because Tom scared me, running into the bathroom and yelling, 'THE WATER MAINS HAVE BURST!' Course, I ran. How was I to know it was a joke?"

I fell over against Albert, hugging myself, the memory was so juicy.

"Hee hee. You should've seen him: sitting bolt upright in the tub with soap-sculptured hair. And then suddenly clambering out to fall sprawling on the bathmat, wet and shiny. Scrambling up yelling 'The water mains've burst!' Tumbling downstairs and helter-skelter out the front door and across the front lawn into the street . . . and then he stopped, panting, his bare legs still pink from the hot water, his washcloth dripping in his fist, looking frantically up and down the street, yelling, WHERE?

WHERE?

      WHERE?

WHERE?

    WHERE?

        WHERE

          WHERE

            WHERE . . . . . .

                WHERE . . . .

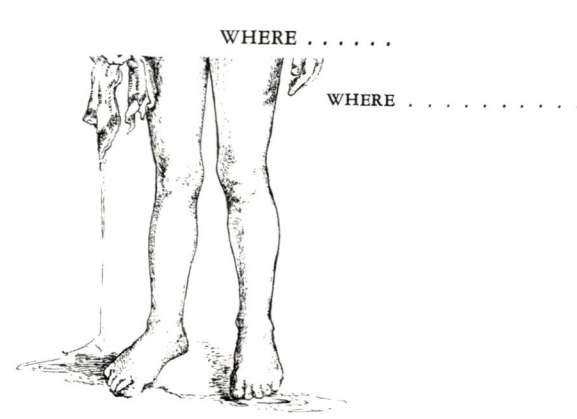

And then he dropped the washcloth and grabbed himself like a fig-leaf, running up the lawn, scrambling under the front porch."

Tim was grinning sheepishly.

"Yeah," said Steve, "and you could hear him all up and down the street, yelling, 'Tom, get me my clothes. Please, Tom,
Tom Tom Tom Tom Tom Tom Tom,

Tom, get my clothes.

TOM, HERE COMES *ALICE*!'

And then silence, till Alice had passed."

"But I saw him," said Alice, looking over the top of the next booth. "Like a mushroom or a ghost in the dimness behind the lattice."

"Then he started up again, threatening, cajoling, yelling, 'Tom, I'll say the dirty word you taught me last week. I'll shout it, Tom, if you don't get my clothes.'

Silence.

'Tom, *please*.

Tom, I'll give you a quarter.

Tom, I'll tell Ma what you did to the milkman last week.

You can throw a towel out on the lawn so I have to run out bare again, Tom. . . . . .

But don't call any girls, Tom.

I hate you, Tom.'

Snuffle, bawl.

'I'm crying, Tom.

> Tom is a nose picker,
> Tom is a nose picker,
> Tom is a nose picker—
> I won't stop till you come—
> Tom is a nose picker,
> Tom is a nose picker.'

Cough, cough.

'I'm catching *cold*, Tom. Maybe there's a tuberculosis beetle hiding in the cobwebs or measling through the dust toward me. Suppose I *die*, Tom?'
. . . till your mother came home and dropped her bag of groceries in the driveway, seeing Tim all of a sudden staring out at her through the lattice like a wildman."

So we all grinned, and I nudged Tim on the shoulder with my fist to show, you know, he was a good kid, taking it like that, not getting mad or anything.

"Hey, Tim," said Joe. "Come on. What was it like finding yourself all of a sudden in the middle of the street with nothing on?"

"Ssah," says Tim, grinning.

"No. Really," said Joe. "Seriously. What'd it feel like?"

Tim sucked at his Coke under his pith helmet.

"Like you're all of a sudden surrounded by wolves and wild boars and cobras, all coming at you, and there's nowhere to turn; you're trapped; you wish it was a dream; the whole world's looking at you, it's homeplate at Yankee Stadium on the Fourth of July, ALL GIRLS!"

Slish slish slish slisssssssssssssssh slish: Tim sucked up the dregs of his Coke. By now it seemed just as hot in the drugstore as it had outside.

"The air conditioner's busted," I said.

"It ain't," said Joe, slovening himself up off the table. "You'll see it ain't. Wait'll you get outside. Here comes old Manson."

Sure enough, there he came, pulling at his warty old ear.

"You boys finished yer Cokes?"

"No Sir." "Almost." "Got a little more in the bottom, Sir."

He surveyed the table, screwing up his mouth.

"Tom Charles," he said to me, "where's yours? You know the rule: 15¢ mini-mum."

"I threw my cup in the trash," I said.

"Mary," he called. "Mary. Did Tom Charles here have the mini-mum?"

She shook her head.

"Out," he said to me. "Out."

"Can't I even wait for the others to *finish*?"

"Out. Out."

So we hauled ourselves up, groaning, and trooped out.

(See *Hot II*, page 38)

The Crocodile

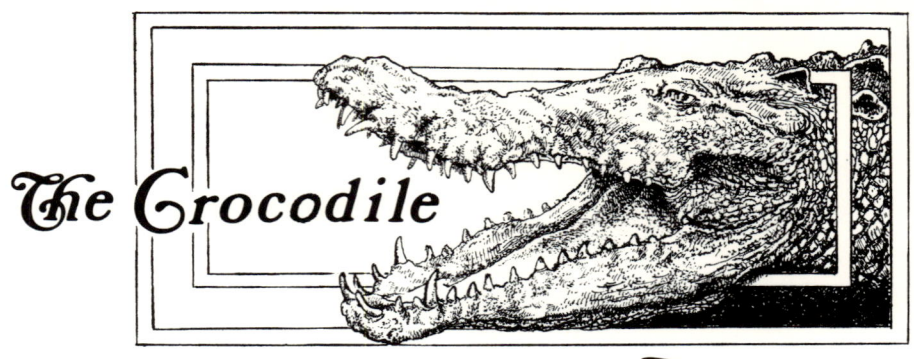

A Story

"Suppose a crocodile," cried Peter, "wandered into the fifth-grade room one morning? CRUNCH! He munches a desk. SQUARK! He tries the blackboard but can't get his jaws around it. CLATTER SPLIT BUNG! He lashes his tail angrily, tumbling chairs and desks into a corner.

"Mrs. Canfield throws him her dictionary and potted geranium, screaming,

'Run, children, run!'

flinging up the windows, tossing him her bookends, boosting Agnes Carter, yanking Tim Wright.

"The crocodile approaches down an aisle, jaws dripping.

" 'Quicker!' she screams, pulling Bob McKeon's jacket over his head as she pushes-pulls him out a window. The croc waddles around Jill Armstrong crouched beside her desk, her arms wrapped over her head, and sashays into the next aisle. Backed against the radiator, Mrs. Canfield throws him her shoes. Tom Mead, teetering on the chalk shelf of the blackboard, clinging with one hand to the wall map of the world, shies erasers at him. He waddles by. Mrs. Canfield flings bales of report cards and What-I-Did-on-My-Summer-Vacation themes at him as he turns and heads for the long coat closet. Inside, in the dimness behind the closed doors, children push and scream among the coats, stumbling over galoshes and umbrellas. Suddenly, the classroom door bangs open and in rushes . . .

(Continued on page 141*)*

Agnes MacPherson
A Daydream

Suppose I was a Duchess?
with a different nose and unskinny knees,
a mink coat, false eyelashes, a yacht,
no homework . . . my mother respectful:
"Not if you'd rather not,
dear, just have some toast.
May I expect you
   home for lunch?"

Or Agrippa,
Empress of Rome!
with a garden
full of orange trees and peacocks,
and a chariot and stallions to whip a-
long the streets . . .
Sometimes I'd pardon
a disrespectful slave,
but sometimes,
reclining
on my alabaster couch,
I'd harden
my gaze.

Then, "Harps!"
   I'd cry.
"Shake your tambourines!"

But now and then, in
spite of the din,
we'd hear his screams . . .

My mother says I'm silly,
but she doesn't understand,
She's never had a nose
which looks manly on my brother,
but-why-couldn't-I-have-had-some-other?

Suppose,
tomorrow morning at ten,
I looked into the mirror,
and there,
staring back,
was:

    Sophia Agnes MacPherson Loren!

Jane Fonda
doesn't enjoy being Jane Fonda
nearly as much
as I would. . . .

    But everybody says
    I have nice eyes.

And Florence Nightingale,
though she had a lumpy nose,
prevailed
over ignorance,
Generals, filth, and scurvy,
succoring the wounded
in the pesthole at Scutari.

Besides,
I've heard that lots of movie stars
looked like peanut-butter jars
at nine or ten . . .
   and then,
fantastically blossomed,
sexy,
lynx-eyed,
rich, blonde and curvaceous . . .

. . . visit my old school,
Mr. Wilkie and the teachers out on the steps,
   beaming and gracious.
The band strikes up!
     The Agnes MacPherson Song!
composed in my honor by Mrs. Ouhl.
Speeches, a banquet . . .
all day long
little girls running
to touch my skirt,
Mr. Blake flirting . . .

THE GREAT DUCK RESCUE
An Eyewitness Report

When I looked out the window at bedtime, our four ducks were gliding in the moonlight round and round the pond, and a thin scum of ice glazed the puddles in the driveway. In the middle of the night I woke and heard a duck quacking and the house creaking in the cold.

Next morning I looked out, and in the center of the silent snowy pond sat our white Pekin duck, quacking weakly. He was frozen solid in the ice, his webfeet splayed out crookedly on either side.

My father sat on the edge of his bed. His hair was tousled. My mother let the curtain fall.

"How can we rescue him, Tom?"

"After breakfast," grunted my father. "Everybody calm down."

But I got my clothes on and went out by the pond and tested the ice with my shoe and tried to poke the duck with a stick. And then Jerry Turner came across the field and helped me pull a long bean pole out from under the shed.

So the front door slammed, and my father mumbled out with his trousers on over his pajamas, zipping up his mackinaw.

"The duck's frozen solid, Mr. Waley," said Jerry.

My father scratched his bristly chin.

The dining room window ground open.

"Can't you poke him free with a pole, Tom?" called my mother. She was in her bathrobe.

"Where's the blue plastic boat?" my father asked me.

My father and Jerry and me pulled it out from under the lawn chairs in the garage. Then my father went off to look for the pole he'd cut last winter to knock icicles off the porch roof with.

Jerry found a rope and threaded it through the nose of the boat. I began to smash the ice with a hoe.

My father came back around the garage dragging a rusty drainpipe.

"We can bust a path in the ice and then you can push me out in the boat and haul me back," said Jerry.

"No," said my father, the drainpipe dragging and clattering behind him. "If anyone's going to fall in, it better be me."

The window ground open.

"Don't let the children fall in," called my mother.

She was holding my baby sister.

"Okay," said my father, "stand back."

And he began to smash the ice, raising the drainpipe high over his head and letting it fall, ka-splush, onto the ice.

The duck quacked, sluthering its webfeet and cocking its head.

"Now," said my father, puffing. He wiped his nose. "Get the boat."

Jerry and me shoved the boat into the pond.

"Hold it tight against the shore."

The window ground open.

"It won't hold you, Tom," called my mother.

My father grinned and waved his hand, stepping unsteadily into the boat. It wobbled and sloshed under him.

"Hold it steady now," he said.

I bit my lip; Jerry's face was red. My father sat down. The back of the boat sank into the mud.

"Hand me the hoe," said my father, reaching back with one arm and gazing straight ahead. "How's it look?"

"You're gonna sink," I said.

"Yeah," said Jerry. "You're gonna sink, Mr. Waley."

Jerry's sister Shirley came running across the snowy stubble.

"Hi."

"Well," said my father uncertainly, glancing down at the dirty waves sloshing over the bow of the boat. "Shove me off."

"You're going to sink, Mr. Waley," said Shirley. "My mother's watching from the kitchen and she said so."

The window ground open.

"It won't hold you, Tom," called my mother.

"Okay," said my father. "It won't hold me."

He stood up unsteadily and then hopped clumsily out onto the bank.

Jerry's younger brothers, Tim and Barney, came running across the field dragging their father's hip boots.

"Our mother says . . ." began Tim breathlessly.

"It's *my* turn to talk!" yelled Barney.

"It ain't!" said Tim. "You asked Ma if we could bring the boots."

"And when she said yes, you cheered: Hurrah! Hurrah!"

"A cheer doesn't count."

"It does."

"Doesn't."

"Thank you both," said my father, taking the boots.

We all watched him pulling on the hip boots. He almost fell over.

"My father rolls the tops down before he tries to put his feet in," said Jerry.

"Oh," said my father and rolled the tops down.

He waded carefully into the pond, using the drainpipe as a pole. The window ground open.

"Jerry," called my mother, "would you come here a minute please."

Jerry ran around the pond reluctantly, glancing back at my father, who was just wading off into the deep water.

I could hear the mud suck and belch at each step my father took. He winced as the icy water lapped over the tops of the boots.

"I'm out as far as I can go," he said, glancing down.

Wobbling, he slid the drainpipe out on the ice. It stopped six inches short of the duck. The duck quacked and sluthered its webfeet. My father began to smash the ice near it.

"Wait," yelled Jerry.

On the other side of the pond Jerry was tying a clothesline around the neck of our turquoise hot water bottle. Tim and Barney and I set off at a run.

Jerry yanked the knot tight.

"Let me throw it first," I yelled.

The window ground open.

"John, let Jerry throw it," my mother called.

Jerry coiled the rope and, clutching the neck of the hot water bottle, swung it round and round. We all watched him silently. He slung it. The hot water bottle slid across the ice, fatbellied and steaming. The duck quacked. The hot water bottle plumped into it, knocking it loose.

We all cheered. The duck's webfeet sluthered frantically on the ice.

"It still can't move," said my father.

"Maybe it's got sprained ankles," said Shirley.

"Ducks don't have ankles," said Jerry.

"How do *you* know?" said Shirley. "You got a U in spelling."

"What's a U stand for?" asked my father.

"Unsatisfactory," said Shirley.

"When I was in school," began my father, "we . . ."

The window ground open.

"Slide it right next to Dab-Dab," called my mother. "Then it will melt the ice and he can swim to shore."

"My turn!" I yelled.

But Jerry pushed me aside and began coiling the rope for another throw.

"Stop it, John," said my father. "Let Jerry throw it once more and then you can try."

But when I tried, the rope got twisted around my leg and the hot water bottle just plopped onto the ice and hardly slid at all.

Jerry grabbed the rope.

"Jerry," called my father, "let John have another turn."

I coiled the rope carefully.

"Come on," said my father, "this water's cold."

He began to smash at the ice with the drainpipe again.

But I let go of the hot water bottle too late and it flew back over my head, jerking me down on my back in the snow.

"That doesn't count!" I yelled, scrambling up. "It didn't hit the ice."

"It does so!" said Jerry, grappling with me.

"John!" yelled my father. "Stop it. You fouled up twice. Let Jerry have a turn."

I kicked the hot water bottle and went over and stood by the porch.

My baby sister stared at me through the window so I stuck out my tongue at her.

Jerry flung the hot water bottle across the ice. The rope slithered out of his grasp and across the ice like a snake.

"Ha, ha," I whispered.

"I lost hold of the rope, Mr. Waley," yelled Jerry.

"He lost hold of the rope," shouted Shirley.

My father waded back to the bank and clambered out.

The duck quacked forlornly out on the ice.

"What are you going to do now, Mr. Waley?" asked Shirley.

We all watched him. He took off his mackinaw and began to empty the pockets of his trousers.

"Your father sure carries a lot of stuff in his pockets," whispered Jerry.

I nodded.

My father slid the boat into the pond and lowered himself gingerly into it. Shirley handed him the hoe. The boat slid gurgling off the bank. My father shoved with the hoe. Water slopped over the sides. He grimaced.

"Oh, he's going to sink," moaned Shirley.

"I bet he won't," said Barney.

"I bet he will," said Tim.

"Won't."

"Will."

We all watched as he pulled and pushed against the ice with the hoe, propelling the boat slowly through the narrow path of open water toward the duck and the steaming hot water bottle.

The window ground open.

"Tom, be careful."

My father paused to let the rocking of the boat subside and then, reaching out, hooked the hoe around the duck and pulled him toward the open water. The duck quacked and sluthered frantically on the ice. Ducks are stupid.

"There," grunted my father. The duck slid into the water. We all cheered. I could even hear Mrs. Turner cheering faintly at her kitchen window across the field.

"Don't forget the hot water bottle," called my mother.

"John, get back from the bank," said my father. "You're scaring him."

"We're not."

"Get back from the bank."

We all backed up. The duck floated in the icy, dirty water, bobbing its head.

"He wants to go upstream where the other ducks are," said my father.

The window ground open.

"He can't climb out, Tom," called my mother.

My father sighed and pulled and pushed himself back toward the bank, the hot water bottle steaming in the bottom of the boat between his legs. The duck scrabbled frantically at the bank. My father clambered out and picked him up.

"His feet look all right."

"Bring him inside," called my mother.

"Oh, poor Dab-Dab," said my mother, taking him.

"He's all right," said my father. "He'd be better off out with the other ducks."

"There's something wrong with his legs."

"Lemme see," I said.

"Stop it," said my mother. "Don't pull at him. Your shoes are sopping. Go upstairs and change."

She set him down on the stone floor. He collapsed, his web feet splaying out under his plump, feathered body. He cocked his head to look at my mother. I started for him.

"Maybe if I hold up his neck he'll . . ."

"John! Stop it. Why can't you ever learn to mind? Upstairs. Now. I want those shoes changed this instant."

She knelt beside the duck.

"Tom, we'll have to put him in a box."

When I came downstairs, the duck was shut up in a cardboard box, scrabbling and quacking softly.

"Shhhhhh," said my mother. "Don't wake him."

"Come outside," whispered my father. "You can help me put the boat away."

"My feet are cold."

"Come on now. We had fun rescuing him. Now we've got to clean up."

Outside, Jerry was dragging the boat back to the garage.

I ran after him.

"I'll help you pull it."

When we went back into the house, the duck was waddling about on the rug, pecking at some kernels of popcorn my mother had put in a paper cup for him.

"I think his legs just got cramped, spread out on the ice all night like that," said my mother.

We all watched him pecking at the kernels of popcorn.

"Ducks are stupid," I said.

CRAZY TOM

WELL, SEE, so there we were, the four of us, Harvey, John, Arlo, and me, trapped on the roof of the old coat factory, five stories up, with Crazy Tom panting and growling and spitting behind the door to the stairs. We could see his eye peering through now this crack, now that, now another. Then he started poking his fingers through, working at the rotten wood, trying to enlarge the cracks.

"It won't do any good to shout for help," whispered Arlo. "It's Sunday. Nobody's around."

We were crouched down behind a stack of old oil drums where we could watch the door.

"And we haven't got any rope," whispered John. "We can't lower anybody down to the fire escape to run for help."

BANG!   BANG!   BANG!   BANG!   BANG!   BANG!

"He's trying to bust in the door!"

We peered through the stack of oil drums. The door bulged every time he hit it.

Harvey put his head down on the tarpaper roof and wrapped his arms over it.

"We gotta have a *plan*!" I yelled over the banging.

"Scatter," yelled Arlo. "We could all scatter. Then he couldn't catch all of us."

Harvey peeked out from under his arms.

"Yeah, but it'll be me. He'll catch me; I know it, I . . ."

I gave him a kick. He shut up, wrapping his arms tighter around his head.

"We could roll oil drums at him when he breaks through," shouted John.

"Shhh," I said. The banging was subsiding. "He'll hear us."

"So what?" whispered Arlo. "He knows we're up here."

Silence.

"Yeah, but he doesn't know where. The only chance we got is to lure him away from the door."

"He's so *quick*," whispered John. "I mean, he's as big as a house, and he shakes all over like jelly when he runs, his arms spread out working at the air, his frog throat wobbling and waggling; his eyes bugging out . . ."

Snorrrrrre. Snorrrrrre.

"What's that?"

"Sounds like snoring."

"Someone go have a look."

"Not me."

"Me neither. Suppose it's a trick?"

"Come on. We'll choose up. Odd man out."

"Darn."

I crept around the stack of oil drums. Behind me I could hear Harvey telling the others all the things Crazy Tom was supposed to have done before he'd been sent away to the asylum: how he'd broke a dog's back with a kick, how he'd thrown Mr. Chisum off Rochester's Bridge into the river. I circled way around and came up on the back of the entryway. He was snoring all right: regular, peaceful, like a Mack truck. I put my eye to a crack. In the dimness inside, streaked with slivers of sunlight, I could see Crazy Tom's huge bulk slumped out on the floor. I counted slowly to 1000, watching him. Then I crept back to the others.

Harvey was against it, but Arlo and John agreed, so Harvey had to go along.

"Keep watching him," I whispered, easing the doorknob around. The door swung slowly open. He hadn't moved. Snorrrrrre. Snorrrrrre. I motioned to John to go first; he motioned to Arlo; Arlo motioned to Harvey; Harvey motioned back; Arlo tiptoed into the entryway, sidled along the wall, stepping gingerly over Crazy Tom's sprawling bare feet. Creeeeeeak! Arlo froze. A rotten board. Crazy Tom groaned and wiped his blubbery, unshaven lips. Arlo waited, hugging himself, then tiptoed on. At the head of the stairs he turned, motioning to us to come on. John. Me. We watched Harvey stepping over the mammoth dirty feet . . . .

"ORRRRRRRRRRGGGGGGGGHHHHHHHHHH!"

(*Continued on page 11,004*)

BONUS! BONUS! BONUS! BONUS! BONUS! BONUS! BONUS! BONUS!

(N.B.: These six bonus pages contain an exciting comic book. However, since the author cannot draw very well, most of the pictures usually found in a comic have been replaced by words.)

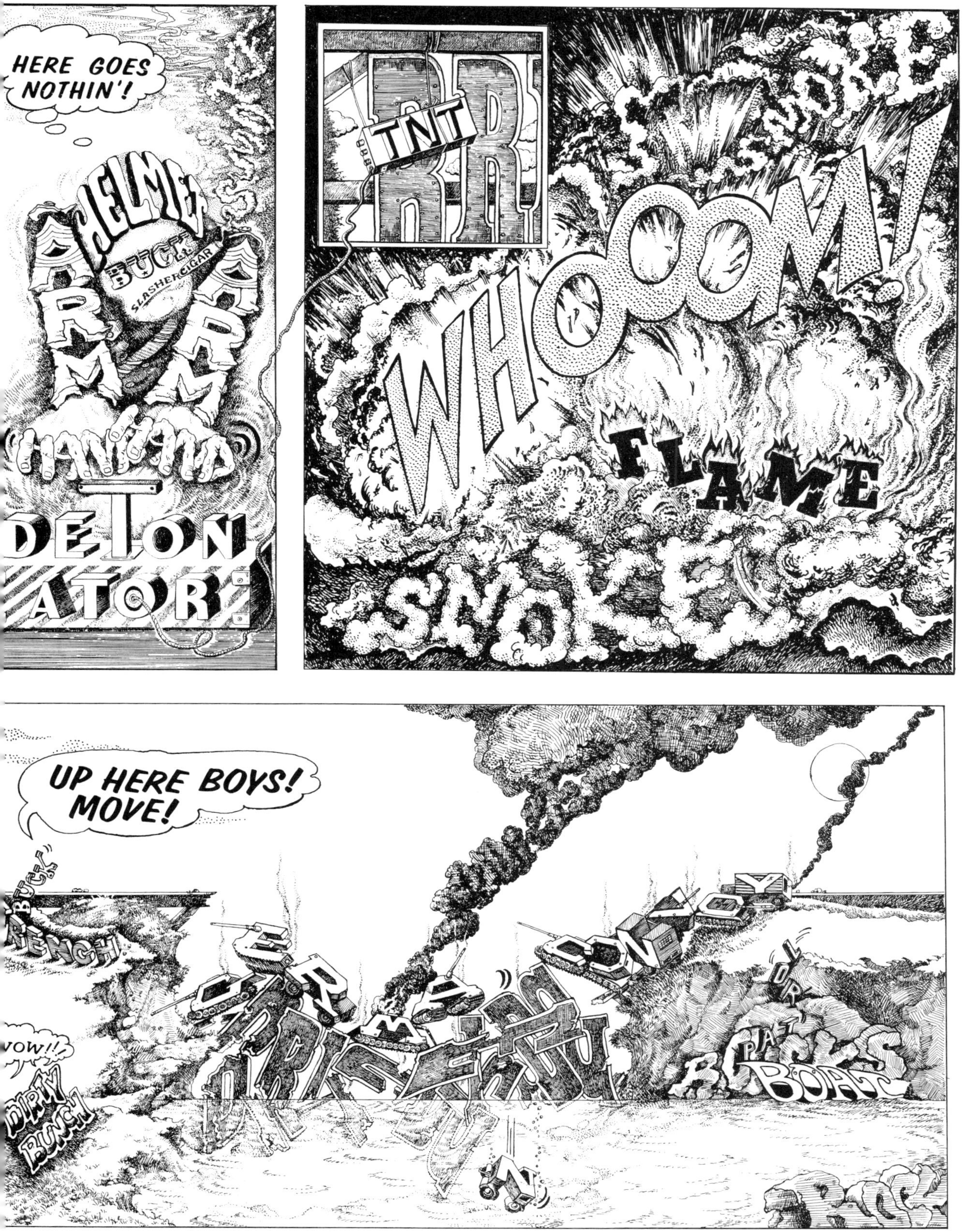

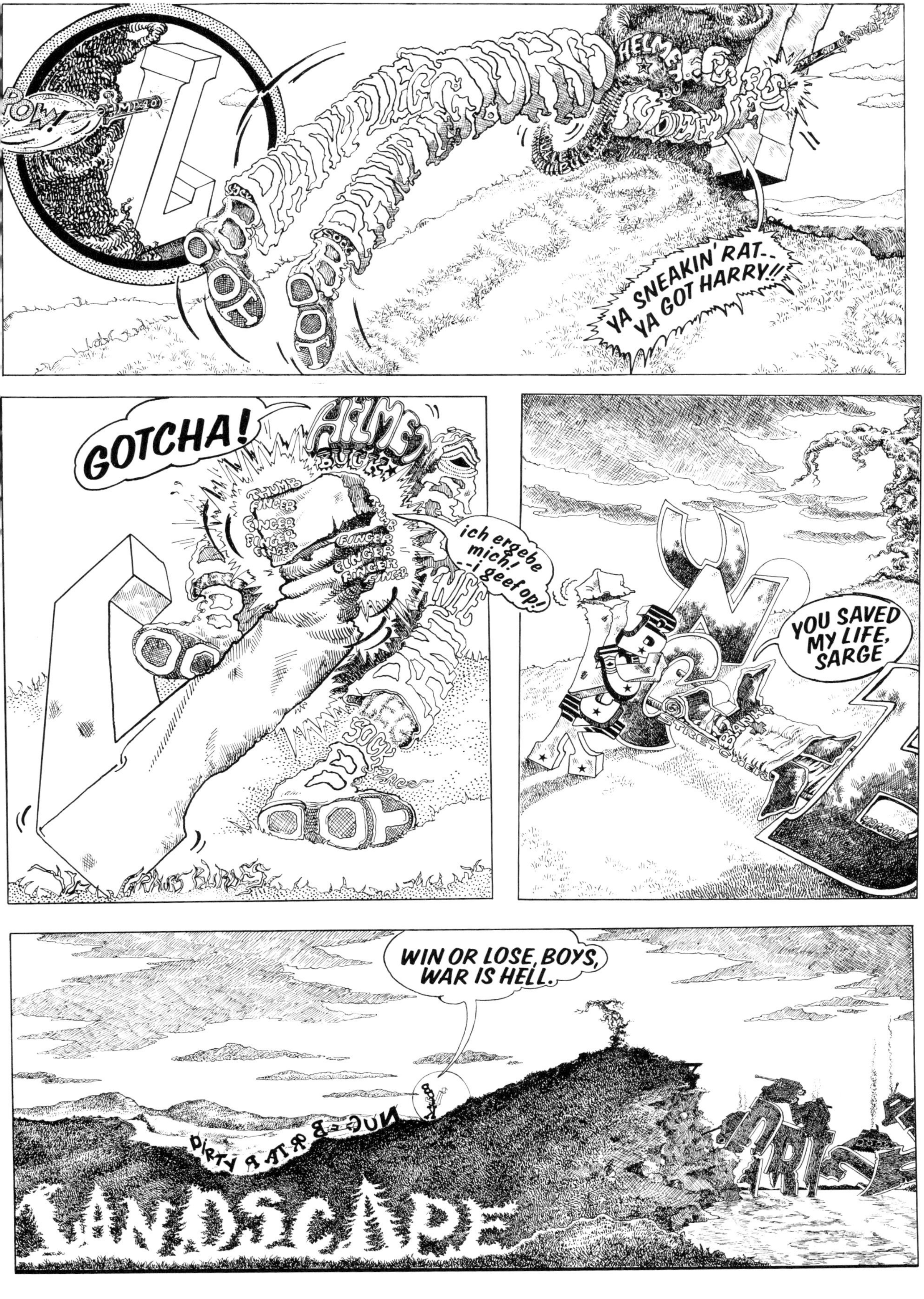

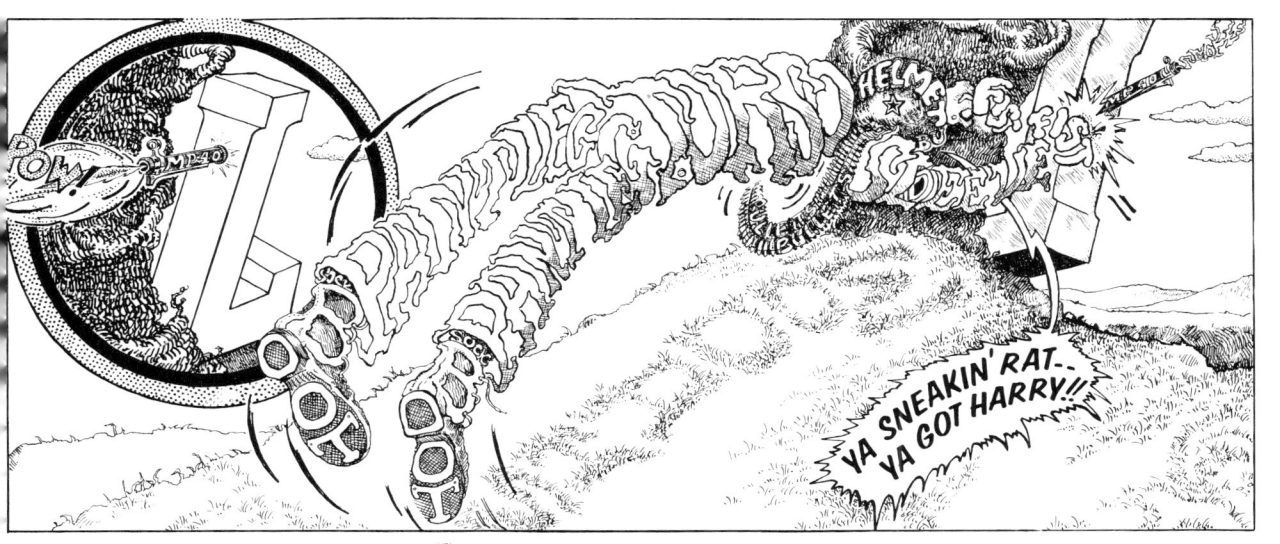

ADVERTISEMENTS!!!   ADVERTISEMENTS!!!   ADVERTISEMENTS!!!

Burglarproof Your House!

Just discovered in the jungles of Mysore! Get a cageful of Warty Indian Lizards. Release them in your living room before you go to bed. Then watch through a peephole as they attack an intruder.
Fierce Biters!   Ravenous Clawers!
They Attack in Packs!
No Known Antidote!
Will Not Harm Furniture or Rugs!
Box 762

Elbow Softener

Do you have rough, unsightly elbows? Send today for a jar of Dr. Jude's patented

ELBOW SOFTENER
Box 2

This is Joe Muscle. Was that you I saw the other day slinking through the weeds behind McInerney's so Bully Tom wouldn't lick you?

HEY, BOYS!

You don't have to be afraid *any* more! I guarantee that IN ONE WEEK you'll be bullying Bully Tom. You'll have

the muscles of an

APE!

All round the neighborhood they'll call you **TNT!** and **WATERLOO!** and **MEAN!** They'll call you **GRISTLE!** and **HAMMER-HAND!** and **BATTLESHIP!** You'll be

*   *
THE ALL-AMERICAN BOY
*   *

Muscles on top of muscles on top of muscles on top of HEART!

HEY, BOYS!

Just fifteen minutes a day! They don't call me Joe Muscle for nothing.

```
Dear Joe:
  Rush me ——— copies of your fabulous
  book: "Muscles by Muscle." Thanks.
NAME
ADDRESS
```

Personal

Dear Joe Reese:
    All is forgiven. Please come home. Your mother and I take back everything we ever said. Your favorite dinner is warming in the oven.
        Signed, Your Daddy.
        Warburton, Ill.

Fool your friends

Slap on one of our artificial scars. They'll all feel sorry, then you'll peel it off and laugh in their faces.
Box 15

INFESTED?

Want to Use Your Living Room Again? If Warty Indian Lizards infest your living room and refuse to leave, even to go to the bathroom, buy a dozen of our Calcutta Vipers, arch-enemies of the Warty Lizards. Feed the vipers through the keyhole, then watch as they attack the noxious lizards.

STAND BACK!

The blood and fur will fly! We do not guarantee you won't be horrified. Widowed ladies should not apply. No money-back guarantee!
Box 762

Are You the Heir to $1,000,000 And Don't Know It?

Fabulous inheritances lie unclaimed in banks all across the country. Where is Joe Reese? $250,000, left him by an uncle, is lying fallow RIGHT NOW in the First National Bank of Warburton, Illinois, because **nobody can find him.** Send $2.00 for a complete listing of names of lost heirs. You, too, can be rich and fancy, wear a fresh carnation in your buttonhole every day! (All names authenticated by National Association of Trust Officers)
Box 4

Battle of Waterloo

Complete, down-to-the-last-detail authentic replica of the famous Battle of Waterloo: Napoleon on his horse, Marshall Ney, the Duke of Wellington, General Grant. 1000 cannons, 2000 hussars, 500 tanks, authentic battle flags.
! ! ! ! ! ! ! Only $1.50 ! ! ! ! ! ! !
Box X

MAGIC BASEBALL BAT

A secret which would destroy the game of baseball as we know it; a secret that owners, players, and equipment managers have spent millions to suppress; a secret which Bowie Kuhn, Commissioner of Baseball, has called "block-busting" and "un-American" can now be yours. Send $10.50 (no stamps please) to JCB, P.O. Box 693, Brooklyn, Neb. Note: please do not reveal this address to any but your closest friends. Organized baseball wants it desperately:

THEY'RE OUT TO SHUT US DOWN

"I was batting .128. Then I sent off for one of your Magic Baseball Bats. Now my average is .571 and it'd be even higher only the pitcher is my brother so I gotta go easy on him."

— J. R. Waxman,
Sioux Falls, N.D.,
Babe Ruth League

XYZ Real Estate

We buy snake- and/or vermin-infested houses. Because our clientele is limited to snake charmers, Indian fakirs and weirdos, we are able to buy and sell houses which ordinary brokers will not touch. Discreet service. No haunteds please.
Box 762

But your mother says you can't have one? We will deliver to your door on a windy, rainy night in early March a cute, six-week-old kitten who has been carefully trained to limp and mew piteously. Guaranteed! $4.50 (comes with tear-inducing Maine onion for yourself)
Box 95.

THE VAMP

Dorrie May,
age 9,
waiting for the school bus,
is more beautiful today
than yesterday:
she's wearing

HOT II: toiletpaper

"WE CAN'T ALL fit in *there!*" said Joe.

"We got to," I said.

Tim poked his head around Joe. We were all in the Men's Room at Grant's, looking into the broom closet.

"Why?"

"Because suppose someone comes in, dumbhead? You want to get kicked out of here and have to go out in that heat again, like at Manson's?"

"Let's *go*," said Albert, who was holding our four boxes of popcorn. "Come *on*."

"Okay, okay," I said. "Tim, you climb up on that shelf; Joe, squirm in behind those brooms and mops; Steve, up on that pail — you can lean back against the wall — me and Albert'll stand."

"That'll leave two pairs of feet showing under the door."

"Naw, we're gonna stand in paper bags. Tim, hand down two of those paper bags."

Albert passed around the boxes of popcorn. I shared my box with Tim. Pretty soon Joe said,

"If somebody comes in, stop chewing. It sounds like there's about *fifty* kids in here eating popcorn."

After a while Steve suddenly laughed and shook his head and said,

"Ha. Geez. Did I ever tell you about what happened to me once when I was in fifth grade? Before I moved here? Geez. Boy." He whistled. "Wait'll you hear this. See,

I was going down the hall at school to the bathroom real worried one day, because I was right in the middle of a history test and I couldn't remember whether Governor Bradford had been the head of the Pilgrims or the Conquistadores. So I was trying to figure it out, walking along, concentrating, scratching my neck, and I shouldered into the Girls' Room instead of the Boys'. The first thing I knew BLAM! I'd smacked into a door post where there should've been nothing, just a row of urinals along the wall ahead of me. I staggered back, sort of stunned, glancing around, wondering what had happened . . . all those *booths*? no urinals? a solid row of *booths*? . . . GIRLS' ROOM! It came to me all of a sudden. I was in the *Girls'* Room! I'd missed the *Boys'* Room!

I looked around for the door. Smacking my head like that, seeing that solid row of booths staring at me — I was sort of dazed, I couldn't remember which way I'd come in. But just as I spotted the door . . . it started to open toward me. I grabbed for a booth, scrambled into it and up onto the toilet (otherwise they'd see my sneakers; none of the girls wore basketball sneakers). Standing on the rim of the toilet, I leaned against the door, latching it, panting. . . .

"I don't know, Mrs. McClendon, I'm sure. And she's such an *unattractive* child."

Teachers! My foot slipped into the toilet, I grabbed for the toiletpaper dispenser on the wall, it dropped open, I toppled backwards KERSPLASH! into the toilet.

Silence. Paper fluttering down all around me.

Then, outside the booth at the sink, a throat was cleared nervously, a faucet shut off.

"Do you suppose the plumbing has *exploded*, Mrs. Henderson?"

"Exploded? Can plumbing explode?"

"It was such a terrible *noise*."

"From the second booth."

Silence. I didn't dare move. Except to silently brush the pieces of toiletpaper off my face.

"I don't see any *water*. Wouldn't it flood if it had exploded?"

"It could be flooding inside the wall. Shall I call Mr. Fitzgerald?"

"Knock on the booth first. Is there somebody in there? Maybe it was just a very violent sneeze or something."

Knock, knock.

If they got Mr. Fitzgerald, it was all up with me. So, sitting in the toilet bowl, covered with toiletpaper, beginning to shiver in the icy water, I says in a high, squeaky voice:

"Yis?"

"Is that you, Mrs. Austen?"

I couldn't say I was Mrs. Austen. Suppose they met her in the hall when they went out?

"No'm, it ain't."

Whispers. Silence. More whispers. It came to me: they couldn't understand why they couldn't see feet under the door of the booth. What could I do? Sneakers were no good. I shucked them off. Socks next. I figured it was my only chance.

My bare feet patted down on the cold tile floor.

"*Oh!*"

"*Mrs. McClendon!*"

Whispers. I could catch a few words now and then: "unusually small . . . gnarled . . . the toe nails . . . Mrs. Speirs? . . ."

And then, aloud: "Mrs. Speirs?"

Geez, she was a wizened-up, white-haired old lady, the school dietitian. Did my feet look as bad as that? I craned my neck to gaze down at them.

"Mrs. Speirs? Is that you?"

High, squeaky voice: "No'm, it ain't."

More whispers. Geez, I was freezing to *death*! My feet on the cold tile floor, my hind end in the icy water. What were they so curious for? Couldn't they give an old woman some peace? And then I heard: ". . . stand on the toilet . . . just peek over the top. . . ." Silence. And then somebody sneaking into the booth beside the one I was in.

I clumb onto the toilet, desperate, as quiet as I could, set my left bare foot on the bracket of the toiletpaper dispenser, grabbed the top of the booth, hoisted . . . my . . . *grunt* . . . self . . . CREAK! I froze.

Squeak of the toilet seat being lifted in the booth beside the one I was in. I had to keep going. I hooked my right bare foot over the top of the booth, elbowed myself up . . . up . . . the sneakers in my shirt scraping against my chest as I squirmed over . . . hung on the other side, my feet groping for the toilet bowl, my socks dangling from my mouth like a walrus mustache . . . *there*! I dropped onto the toilet, safe.

From the next booth, an astonished voice: "There's *no one* in it! It's empty!"

"It *can't* be!"

"It is."

"Are there any signs of anyone? Shoes? Clothing?"

"Just toiletpaper. Scattered *all over*."

The door of the booth rattled.

"But the door's locked from the inside."

Squeak of a toilet seat.

"We just must get to the bottom of this."

"Is the next booth locked?"

Rattle rattle.

"Yes."

"We can stand on this wastebasket."

Over I went: toilet bowl, dispenser, top of the booth, hang . . . drop.

"Empty."

"Try the next."

Over I went: toilet bowl, dispenser, top of the booth, hang . . . drop.

"Try them all."

Up and over. Up and over. Up and over. Four times. Till I crouched on the seat of the last booth, panting hard, rubbing my sore hands. The wastebasket clanked down outside the booth. Over I went, back the way I'd come, blowing.

"Nothing."

"All empty?"

"Not a sign of anyone."

"Well, we *both* saw the feet. There must be *someone*."

"Could it have been an optical illusion?"

"The two feet *I* saw were very real and dirty-looking."

"Perhaps it was a sort of mass hallucination. You know, like the kind you read about in the *Reader's Digest*?"

"Were you thinking about feet when it happened? I was still wondering what to do about Sarah Meehan."

"Well, Sarah does have very large feet. Have you ever noticed? Her loafers must be size eight."

"I sup-*pose* it . . . what were you thinking about?"

"I'd rather not say."

"Oh come, Mrs. Henderson."

Stiff voiced: "It was personal . . ."

"Well, I'm sure I'd be the last . . ."

". . . and private."

"As you wish."

Sound of water running. Gloop and clatter of soap dispenser.

"Would you care for a towel, Mrs. Henderson?" (*Very* hoity-toity.)

"Thank you."

Click click click click click. High heels up the tile floor. Whoosh . . . siiigh of door. Mutters at sink: "I *never* . . . stiffnecked old ——— . . . couldn't teach her way out of a paper bag . . ."

Click scrape, click scrape, click scrape. She must have a busted heel. Whoosh . . . siiigh. I dropped down off the toilet bowl, sat, flinging on socks, sneakers, and toppled back SPLASH again! *Geez*. Puff.

I heaved up . . . heaved . . . HEAVED!!! It couldn't be! I was stuck! I couldn't get free. I was wedged into the toilet seat! Whoosh . . . siiigh. Helen Sligsby, the worst tattle-tale in the school. I figured I'd better sit tight, trust to luck the next one in wouldn't be a teacher.

I pulled my shirt collar up, hung my head down. Maybe Helen wouldn't notice I was a boy. I couldn't even reach the door to shut it. Geez, was the water *cold*. Helen skipped scuffing back up the aisle.

Whoosh . . . siiigh. Safe. Whew.

Whoosh . . . siiigh: Annemarie Foster. She'd scream bloody murder. Faucet running, bonk in the pipes. Boy, was I *stuck*. I couldn't even *wriggle* hardly. I stared down at the white tile floor, at my feet, one sock on, one half off. Whoosh . . . siiigh.

If the next one in wasn't someone I could trust, I'd die of the cold. How could I go back to class all wet anyway? Whoosh . . . siiigh. *Jane Cummings and Sylvia Cohen*! GEEZ! I mean I knew I could trust them; they wouldn't tell on me. But, geez, I'd never hear the end of it. I'd be giggled at and teased for a week. They'd *never* let up.

But what could I do? I had to get unstuck before the period ended and the whole bathroom filled up with screeching girls.

"Hey, Jane," I whispered.

They were chattering and primping at the mirror, must have finished the history test early.

"Hey, Jane."

"Who's that?"

"Shhh. Come here."

Footsteps.

"STEVE!?! What are *you* doing in here?"

Jane backed out of the doorway.

"Shhh. Quiet. Someone'll hear. I'm stuck. You got to pull me out before someone comes."

Whispers. *Geez!*

"How'd you get stuck?"

"And what were you doing in here anyway?"

"Geez, I was *thinking*, you know, the test and all, and I didn't look where I was going and then Mrs. McClendon and Mrs. Henderson busted in so I hid and now I'm *stuck*. You got to help me out before the bell rings!"

I was desperate. You know. And they'd begun to giggle.

More whispers.

"Jane, will you *help me out*, for cripes sake?"

More giggles.

"Are you decent?"

"Of course I am. I *fell in*. By *mistake*."

They appeared in the door, giggling, Sylvia on tiptoe behind Jane, craning her neck to look at me trapped in the toilet bowl. Then they both collapsed against each other, laughing helplessly.

I was so desperate, red-faced, trying to heave myself unstuck, I couldn't contain myself — I shouted,

"FOR CRIPES SAKE, WILL . . ." and then remembered where I was and hissed, "I'll get you for this. You think I won't but I will."

They collapsed back against the wall, weeping with laughter. I suppose I *was* a sight — a spider pinned to a board — waving my arms about and kicking and lunging and heaving, hissing pleas and threats at them, grunting, moaning. The class bell braaannged. I gave a final, desperate, dying, cornered LUNGE!

      and came free, barreling through the door of the booth, spun around by the jamb, piling into Jane and Sylvia, trying to-scramble-up-tangled-in-weeping-giggling-girls . . . and burst out of the Girls' Room . . . free

      FREE!

   free

     into the hall.

Around the corner, tumble slide down the stairs, BANG through the gym doors, slide crash fling open the door, and
    down
     to
      the
       safety
        of
         the
          locker
           room,

where I sat for ten minutes in the bottom of my locker, recovering — panting and sighing and pushing the hair off my sweaty forehead. Then I took off my pants and wrung them out as best I could, pulled them on again, tied two sweatshirts around my waist to hide some of the wet and snuck out through a window and went home.

"What'd your mother say?"

"She was coming out of the laundry room and caught me climbing in the cellar window. I told her some high school kids had pushed me down in a puddle. " 'Out with it,' she says, setting the basket of laundry down on the stairs. 'You wouldn't be climbing in the cellar window, young man, if some boys had pushed you down in a puddle.'

"So I started fumbling along, trying to fudge some of the essential points, like it was the Girls' Room, but she kept catching me up, so finally I gave in and spread myself all out before her. I wouldn't have had much chance anyway, she was always talking to Sylvia Cohen's mother on the telephone. When I was about halfway through, she sat down sideways on the stairs with her back to me, folding the laundry — I was by the furnace — and pretty soon I saw her shoulders begin to shake. When I come to Mrs. Henderson saying maybe the feet were a mass hallucination like in the *Reader's Digest*, she laughed right out and after I'd finished, she took me upstairs and cut me a slice of cake big enough to choke a horse. I had to tell the whole thing all over again to my father when he came home, and he laughed so hard he spurted pea soup all over the tablecloth. I was glad they weren't angry, you know, but geez, if they thought it was *that* funny, they were sure to tell it every time they went out to dinner. So when Mom came to tuck me in that night, I asked her not to tell anybody. 'But, Steve,' she says, 'it's so funny. And Sylvia and that other girl are sure to tell their friends about it.' 'Please, Mom?' I says. So she said all right, she wouldn't. And then at breakfast the next day my father promised. Because I was really upset: you know, everybody'd tease me and laugh at me when I got to school. I was in torments on the bus.

"But it didn't turn out so bad. Sylvia and Jane had told everyone, of course, but they didn't know how I'd got into the Girls' Room or what I was doing there, so they were all a little puzzled. I went around looking mysterious and nodding significantly. When someone laughed or kidded me, I'd say, 'Laugh. Go ahead. You'll see.'

" 'What'll we see?'

" 'You wait. You'll see.'

"So then they'd look sort of queer, as if they'd just had a gas pain, and pretty soon the teasing would peter out. And the next day I pretended I was sick and stayed home in bed, reading comic books Bill smuggled in to me, and the day after that a kid fell off the roof of the equipment shed in the playground before school and broke his collarbone, so I was pretty well forgotten."

"I always wondered what Girls' Rooms were like," said Albert.

"They're nothing," said Steve. "You know, just a row of booths exactly like the ones in ours, noth ———"

CRASH!

We all tumbled out in a heap onto the floor of the Men's Room at Grant's.

"Awright

awright

awright

awriiiiiiiiiight," says a voice. "What is this? A pack meeting?"

We looked up. Eddie Bowles was glaring down at us, one hand on the knob of the broom closet door. He was the center on the high school basketball team. Grant's had hired him as a summer security guard.

We untangled and stood up, grumbling.

"Let's go, let's go," says Eddie. "Move along there. The heat'll do you good. We ain't running a country club for hot seventh graders, you know."

We shuffled past cut-rate dresses, past blouses, past the candy counter, like a chain gang of condemned prisoners, through a cash register, out into the . . .

(See *Hot III*, page 60)

mystery page

TWO BONUS PAGES!

(N.B.: These two bonus pages contain an exciting Contest.)

A STAR SPANGLED CONTEST

Open only to readers of
The Portmanteau Book.

Complete, in twenty words or less, the following sentence:

I like **The Portmanteau Book** because ....

Sample answers:

it is not made of plastic.

it is not named Charlie Brown.

my parents hate it.

it is banned in Boston.

it doesn't make ugly noises at me when I roll over on it in bed.

Bebe Rebozo hates it.

it is not in the school library.

my grandmother has never read it.

one of the words in it has a sextuple a.

it is not sold in Woolworth's.

Janie Miller has never even *heard* of it.

my father wrote it.

it is full of sin.

it burns.

my cat likes to sit on it.

it's the same size as the caster I lost off my bed so now I sleep straight again.

it doesn't ask to share my toys and candy.

the author is handsome and intelligent.

it smells good.

you can take it to the beach without caring if it gets wet or sandy or a Frisbee thrower steps on it. *DISQUALIFIED*

you can't eat it, and with my mother, the way she is — "Eat, eat, eat" — that's something.

you can't play catch with it, and with my father, the way *he is*, "Whatta ya say, kid (punch), how's about a little game of ball?" — that's something.

it isn't purple with yellow stripes.

the paper is Grade A spitball.

my teacher likes it.

my teacher doesn't like it.

it cures warts.

it doesn't list the principal exports of Poland.

it can be used as a ruler.

the author is kind to animals.

I traded it to Lonny Simmons for her father's fish knife.

my Scout master says it isn't square and honest and All-American.

the librarian always suggests four other books when you ask for it.

it isn't written in Latin.

you can read it while you're eating spaghetti because you don't care if sauce spatters all over it.

it doesn't have a plot so if the teacher asks you what it's about, you can just say, Life, and get away with it.

you can read parts of it sdrawkcab.

my Aunt Mable and Uncle George didn't think I'd like it.

it isn't anything at all like *Ivanhoe*.

Shirley Steinfeld says it bit her.

the last word in it is zymurgy.

I got an A+ on a book report I did on it.

it has wide margins I can use to draw on when my mother locks me in my room without any paper.

it will never happen again.

I hit Edward Watkins in the stomach with it and he threw up all over the lawn.

Magnificent prizes will be awarded for the best entries. Just mail your entry with four bubble gum wrappers to:

Little, Brown and Company
34 Beacon Street
Boston, Massachusetts 02106

Then sit back and wait for your prizes.

(All entries must be postmarked not later than March 13, 1933.)

STILTON CHEESE AND SILENCE and Other Poems...

Onions in the Ice Cream

Mrs. Creester, blinking,
fell to thinking.
        Sinking
deeper and deeper into her thoughts,
she heated the baby
and changed its bottle,
sneezed in the stew
and salted the sink,
washed the ice cream,
set the baby on the table,
said, "There's stew for dessert,
John, eat your cake."
dried the leftovers
and put the knives in the icebox,
brushed Joanie's hair
and unbuttoned John's pajamas,
put the dog to bed
and let out Eddie,
then slumped down in a chair
in the kitchen, crying,
  "O dear, O dear,
can it be last Tuesday
    already?"

MACHINERY

Generator, pile-driver, fan-belt, squeaks:
I slumped in a packing crate, sweat trickling down my cheeks.
Gasworks, foundry, refinery, mill town:
through the August haze, the sun glared down.

Riveter, planer chuck, lag-screw, cutter:
from far away came a rumble and mutter.
Countershaft, compressor, fuel pump, cleat:
the noise grew to a roar; I ran into the street.

Blast furnace, hose coupling, valve, kerosene:
up the street toward me waddled a huge machine.
Turbine, lug-wrench, four-barreled choke:
pistons driving, cranes hoisting, it puffed greasy smoke.

Anvil, stove bolt, hydraulic beam punch:
right in the center a stamping press munched.
Polishing head, grinder, blow torch, dies:
above it two searchlights blinked like eyes.

Turning mill, crank pin, bolt dog, heat:
as it manufactured toward me, it rumbled clattering, "EAT!"
Diesel engine, dynamo, lathe, caulking gun:
I was so scared, I couldn't run.

Valve, flange, manifold, single-geared shaper:
suddenly out of its side, a fly-wheel capered.
Drive-shaft, bolt-cutter, rachet, oil leak:
the two searchlights exploded; gears clashed and
    shrieked.

Sparkplug, boiler, wrench, two-wheel cart:
the lumbering machine began to fall apart.
Suspension drill, roller bearing, carburetor, screw:
into the sky flocks of rivets flew.

Five o'clock quitting time, men stream out the gate:
I woke up in the packing crate.
Grimy windows dark, a watchman plodding:
I felt like a handful of old crankcase wadding.

Rows of silent machinery, a repair half done:
I trudged home through the setting sun:
foundry, windlass, pneumatic gun.

THE LAME LEFT FIELDER

Andrew End
fell off the South Bend
Young Men's Christian Aid Society's Clubhouse roof.
But it wasn't the end
for Andrew, only a beginning
because he fell into the thirteenth inning
of the Rotary-International-Chamber-of-Commerce-League playoff,
bouncing from the backstop
onto the pitcher, catcher, left fielder, shortstop,
and second baseman, who were discussing whether or not
to dust off
the next batter.
It didn't matter
after that because Andrew ended the game.
The left fielder was lame,
the shortstop's sprained
ankle made him late
to school for a week, and after the catcher
had extricated himself from the pitcher's
shirt, it took him until ten minutes after eight
to get his mask off the second base-
man's face.

SUPPOSE

Eat your peas.

Suppose I sneeze?

Eat your peas!

He sneezed.

The peas
like starlings
soared and swooped
about the room, tinkling
in the chandelier, tarring
the tablecloth and plates, blinking
into the soup.

Eat your calf's
liver.

Suppose I laugh?

Eat your calf's
liver!

He laughed.

The liver
quivered
through the air,
swerved round his father's chair,
and was snagged
by the leaping cat
and dragged
into the closet.

Eat your squash.

Suppose I cough?

Eat your squash!

He coughed.

The squash
like an orange eagle
flew once around the table,
globs streaming out behind,
and vanished through the window,
returning by the door
to splosh
along the floor.

Eat your ice cream.

Suppose I scream?

Eat your ice cream!

He screamed.

The ice cream
like a comet
climbed through the chandelier,
whirled west
around his mother,
swooped north
to circle his father,
drove south
toward his sister,
and then l ͏o͏ ͏o͏ ͏p͏ ͏e͏ ͏d
back into his mouth.

MENU

Hey, let's eat Larry
for supper tonight.

Aw, he's too hairy.

How about Ginny?
She's too skinny.

How about Hugh?
He'd be good in stew.

How about Polly?
She's too jolly.

How about Dudley?
He's too ugly.

How about Gerty?
She's too dirty.

How about Ruthy?
She's too goofy.

How about Gus?
He'd tell on us.

How about Davy?
He'd be good with gravy.

How about Fat Tim?

Bob and Bill ran to catch him,
while Jane scrubbed
out the washtub,
and Anne fetched butter,
salt, and pepper.

Fat Tim had poached a pecan pie
and broiling in the playground sun,
was eating it and swinging.

When told that he was wanted to be baked
for supper, he stewed
and simmered, swinging,
and then boiling
over, cried:

"Oog log ro fug I'll
tood your eyes,
you sogs!" He roasted them
with curses and candied them
with dirt; he kneaded them
with both his fists and basted them
with sticks until they rose
like muffins and ran home drizzling tears.

That evening
Bob
had cod,
Bill
dill
pickles, Anne
ham,
and Jane
tears on a wet pillow
because her mother'd seen her climbing
the willow
tree that morning.

But Fat Tim
ate ham hocks swim-
ming in rich curdled cream,
and steam-
ing cabbage soup,
roast Texas beef, a double scoop
of mashed potatoes,
peabeantomato
pie,
floating i-
sland,
a dish of sugared cherries,
grapes and strawberries . . .
                        and then
he started over,
munching nuts,
gorging on a clover-
fed young gamboling lamb,
Rotterdam
herring, broiled salmon,
veal pie,
       and so on . . .
       and so on . . .
       and so on . . .

Strawberry?

Dorothy Lamb
fell into the jam
and was carried off
by 5,492,633 flies.

Her mother sighed
and opened another
jar for Dorothy's brother.

TRAVELING

Alsace-Lorraine:
here comes a train.

Wilmington, Delaware:
I never go anywhere.

Ancient Rome:
I just sit home.

Boston and Ipswich!
suppose I was rich?

Iraq, Tibet:
I'd buy a jet.

Scapa Flow:
my mother'd say no.

Lincoln, Nebraska:
I wouldn't ask her.

Cape of Good Hope:
I'd visit the Pope.

Strait of Belle Isle:
climb the Sphinx, sail the Nile.

Tokyo, Nome:
once a year I'd come home.

Mississippi, Platte, Moose:
there goes the caboose.

Wilmington, Delaware:
I never go anywhere.

The slums of Baltimore:
I-guess-I'll-go-have-a-soda-at-the-drugstore.

How the Pronouns Fell Out while the Nouns Were Away

Says *I* to *me*
if you was I
then I'd be me.

No, says *me* to *I*.
If you was me
then me'd be I.

But *you*
took a different view.

So *us*
made a fuss.

And *yours*
wasn't sure.

While *he*
and *we*
quarreled in the dictionary.

But *them*,
they and *it*
didn't care a bit.

And *her*
and *his* were
in the kitchen
ordering *his'n*
and *her'n*
about.

While *our*
and *him*
were playing cards
with *antonym*
and *synonym*
in the garden.

In the end
the clamor
work *grammar*,
who hurried downstairs
and made them all sit on chairs
in different rooms
till the *nouns*
came home.

Stilton Cheese and Silence

I.

John Gore
swore.

If his slice of ham
slid off his plate,
he cried, "O d — n!"

If his wad
of gum was stolen
from the gate
at school, he roared, "O G–d!"

If he stubbed his swollen
toe against the sink,
he punched his mother's hip
and screeched, "You f — k!"

If he tipped
his sister's cup
of soup onto her dress,
he bawled, "S — t up!"

Then the Reverend Arthur Binner
came to dinner.

A mess
of jam
glooged
off John's
knife on-
to the floor. He cried, "O d!"

The word caught in his throat.
He choked
and rose
half out of his chair;
his face turned white as cod;
he croaked, "O G!"

The word stuck in his nose.

His mother glared.
His sister cried, "It isn't fair,
he always ruins everything. It's up
to you to discipline him, mother,
you're his parent."
                He choked, "O s!"

The words clogged up his ears,
his tongue turned black as ink,
he mouthed, "You f!"

It lodged beside the others.

II.

The Doctor peered
into his nose. "A singular yet
simple case. If I recall
correctly: suffacosis maledictum."

John sprawled
like a waterlogged worm
on the carpet.

"With rest and castor oil and liver —
taken raw,
with Stilton cheese and silence,
he'll recover."

Ever after
when John burned
with anger, he bawled,
"One!
Two!
Three!
Four!
Five!

Six!

Seven!

Eight!

Nine!

Ten!

Eleven!

Twelve!

durn"

HOT III: UNDERWEAR

. . . heat like a runaway moving van thundering downhill toward a crowded intersection; like an elephant sitting down on your head. We staggered and lolled up the street. The heat was like a jungle; you had to push your way through it — trees, houses, telephone poles bleached and shimmering around you, no bird call, cricket's chirp. Deep down in the cracks of the sidewalk panting beetles hung their heads, beaten down by the heat.

"It's an attack by the Orbs," said Albert, sprawling helplessly against a telephone pole. "They're using their new heat-ray gun. Bammo! Swoooooooooosh! Up goes the Hurtgen Forest. Again! Norway's a cinder, everybody running around with no clothes on, just a few charred shreds flapping in the breeze."

We lunged collapsing into Carl Schurz Park and spread-eagled on our backs in the shade of the Abraham Lincoln maple.

"How come everybody wasn't burnt up along with their clothes?"

"Dial-o-matic aiming. The Orbs can't only hit anything they want anywhere in the world, as small as a pea, as big as the Coliseum in Los Angeles, they can burn as deep or as shallow as they want. Like they can burn the crust off a hotcross bun and leave the inside still yellow and fluffy. So they were out to conquer the earth, country clubs, oil tanks, jimson weeds, and all."

"Why?"

"The planet Orb was rotting like an onion: on one side of it, sickly green sprouts were shooting up, curling and writhing, wreaking destruction and panic in Llemson, the land of the noseless people. On the other side the planet was withering and shriveling, turning a dry yellow in some places, a damp fetid black in others, causing confusion and hunger in Wollaws, the land of the throat-eyed people. And so," said Albert, lying back in the grass with his hands behind his head, gazing up into the cloudless blue sky through the leaves, "and so an expedition to conquer the earth was got up and given a rousing send-off, with speeches and beer, at the 'Orborange Borbowl' in downtown 'Morbiami.'

"They landed in Spitzbergen on the northern coast of Norway and immediately set about melting the polar ice cap, thereby raising the level of the seas by eighty-five feet in three hours and forty minutes and drowning 999,000,000 people between Reykjavik, Iceland and Calcutta, India, where the sea foamed through the streets as if all the lemmings who'd ever run into the sea were coming back out again."

"Hey," I said interrupting, "is this one of your father's stories or one of yours?"

"His," said Albert.

"Okay," I said, because Albert's father tells great stories, but Albert's stories are always just one endless bloody battle after another. It gets dull. He wants to be a writer like his father, but all he's interested in is war.

"Anyway," said Albert, "after a while the Orbs quit melting the ice cap because they didn't want to do in everybody, just make a little room for themselves. The rest of the people they wanted alive, for slaves. So they adjusted the 'Grorbeat OrbarmyNorbavyOrbairforce' gun and burned the clothes off everybody who was left in Norway.

But it was a gray, cold day in April, an icy wind blowing out of the northeast off what was left of the ice cap, and half the people caught the flu and the other half was too stiff with cold and goose pimples to be of any use, so the Orbs packed up their whole show and flew to Los Angeles, leaving the Norwegians trying to get warm under heaps of snarling huskies or prickly fir boughs, plaiting hay skirts and quarreling over who'd get to sit in the hot springs at Trondheim next.

"My father and I'd gone to see the Dodgers play the Mets at Anaheim that day. I was just finishing my third box of popcorn and wondering if I should ask my father to buy me one of those Dodger pennants that were being hawked up through the crowd by a vendor; Tom Seaver was winding up to pitch three and one to Ron Fairly — two out in the last of the seventh. . . .

Thunder rumbled, lightning flashed in the clear, blue sky; the sunlight dimmed. We all looked up, even Tom Seaver and the batter, the plate umpire yelling, 'Balk! Balk!' and there, over the stadium, so monstrous you could only see a tiny rim of blue sky around it, a glowing silver disk hovered, neon lights blinking: dash dash, mostly white, a few red, blue; blunk blunk, wheeooo, sha. The pennant in the vendor's hand flamed up, consumed in a second to a charred stub of a stick, a wisp of smoke.

"Put on your hat, Albert!" yelled my father. "Button your collar!"

And suddenly sirens sounded, bells clanged, buzzers, car horns, factory whistles, rattle thwonk of pile drivers, roar of motorcycle engines, burglar alarms, electrical wheeooooo's, a bedlam of sound . . . . . . dying away the next instant.

Silence.

Silence.

The great disk hovered over the stadium, neon lights flashing . . . And suddenly a blast of intense, white light blanketed the whole stadium, bleaching grass, faces, flags a fish-belly-white; the whole stadium a washed-out color snapshot . . . . zzzzzzzzzzzzzzzzzzzzzzzzzzzzzzzzzzz zzzzzzzzzzzzzzzzzzzzzzzzzzzzz

DARKNESS!

. . . as if everybody had suddenly been struck blind. Thick, pitchy blackness. Not a glimmer or crack anywhere.

And then...

daylight again, the flags waving, a scrap of paper rolling across the outfield grass, the sky overhead cloudless, blue. A man screamed. I felt a cold wind on my legs, glanced down...

I was in my underwear!

My clothes were gone!

What was I gonna do?

"Pop?"

"Pop?"

I was too embarrassed to look up at him, just touched his hairy knee and... *Hairy knee?*... No trousers? He'd lost all his clothes, too!

"Pop," I says, out of the corner of my mouth. "Look. We've lost our clothes. What'll we do?"

"Don't move," he mutters, his chin scrounged down against his chest. "I don't know. I'm trying to think."

So I waited.

"Pop, somebody's gonna *notice*."

"Get up," he mutters, "and walk to the nearest ramp. Don't look around. Don't run. Just walk. I'll follow you."

I stood up in my bare feet, scrunching through popcorn, candy wrappers, Crackerjack cartons, and started down the aisle, not looking up, stepping over one set of bare feet, another, a hairy leg, a... HEY! I glanced up... into a stunned, staring, hambone face! He'd lost all his clothes, too! sitting there dazed in a pair of red-flowered underdrawers and a yellow undershirt, his stomach bulging hairily through the gap. I looked around. EVERYONE! The whole of Anaheim Stadium was in its underwear! 54,963 people in their underwear! Silent, dazed in the sunlight. A wisp of smoke trickling up here and there. Tom Seaver and the other players looking down at themselves in amazement. The plate umpire trying to crouch down behind his chest protector.

"Everybody's like us! Pop, *everybody's* lost their clothes!"

A confused murmur grew across the stadium. Shouts. Crashes. "Help, help!" A shot. Another. The stadium police were firing wildly into the empty sky. The scoreboard went crazy, lights flashing, blinking, running up and down, one to ten, one to ten, Out, Error, Safe, spelling nonsensical words, *squark*! lights blowing out: spluff spluff, spluff spluff spluff. I grabbed my father's hand. People were jumping up, yelling, gesticulating. The big hairy man shook his fist at the sky.

"Come on," my father yelled over the din. He shoved around me and started for the ramp. I followed, half-dragged, half-running. We plunged down the ramp. Behind us the scoreboard exploded. The players were running for the dugouts. The loudspeakers blared,

"Remain calm, remain calm, cremain ralm."

We dashed down the ramp through the running crowd in its underwear: fat men panting along, their great bellies and thighs bouncing soggily; hairy, sun-tanned brutes shouldering aside skinny, pale men, eyes wide with fear behind gold-rimmed glasses. Kids screaming for their fathers, falling, stepped on, kicked, crawling to the walls, clambering up, running on; here and there a woman running in her slip, screaming with indignant embarrassment; gangs of teen-agers fighting through the crowd, dropping off the sides of the ramp onto the level below.

"In here," says my father. He dragged me through a door into a Men's Room and, letting go of me, jumped up on a sink and yanked open the narrow window above it. He stuck his head out.

"Okay," he says, still breathing hard, dropping down off the sink. He lifted me onto the sink and clambered up himself. "Now remember. Just relax when you hit. Don't stiffen up. Okay? Like the paratroops?"

I nodded.

He lowered me out, down, down, down, his face red and straining above me, against the blue sky.

"Now," he says and let go.

My fingers clawed down his wrists, fingers, I glimpsed the sunlit concrete thundering up toward me.

"Limp," I thought, "go limp."

Squash, I sprawled on the concrete.

"You okay, Albert? Albert? *Albert*! You okay?"

I got up, shaking my wrist, feeling my right knee. He was leaning half out of the window.

"Albert?"

"Yeah. I'm okay. My arm . . ."

"Get back. I'm coming down."

He disappeared, a moment later his feet wriggled out the window. Screams, angry bellows came from the gate farther down the stadium wall. Men trickled out of it, running toward the parking lot, the sun gleaming on their bare backs and torn undershirts. My father hung from the window . . . dropped . . . *splug*.

"Ow!"

He scrambled up, twisting to look at his skinned thigh.

"Let's go."

He grabbed my hand. We ran for the parking lot.

And suddenly, from the clear blue sky, a huge hollow voice echoed.

"Norbow horbear thorbis! Norbow horbear thorbis! Yorbou horbave borbeen corbnquered borby thorbe Orbs. Yorbou orbare norbow orbour slorbaves. Morberitorious corbonduct worbill borbe rorbewarded. Morbisbehavior worbill borbe porbunished. Rorbeturn torbo yorbour horbomes orband orbawait orbinstructions."

The voice moved away through the sky. As we ran on past the rows of parked cars, I could hear it somewhere in the distance, repeating its message. We flung into the car. The engine roared; we lurched back, plunged forward, crash-screech, my father jockeying the car wildly, fenders crunching, *zooooooom*! We roared down the aisle between the parked cars, skidded onto the exit ramp, people in their underwear jumping up on car fenders out of our way, shaking their fists at us, cursing. *Screeeeeech* onto the freeway, *screeeeeeeeeeeeeeech bump-bump-bumpety* over the center median and streaking south toward Alhambra, weaving through the wrecks and stalled cars.

After about a mile the wrecks thickened; other cars were trying to pick a way through. We were in a ragged line now, working south, the line coagulating, slowing, slowing, bumper to bumper, stop. Inch ahead. Stop. A man in a bathing suit was standing on top of a car bunged against a light post near us.

"How's it look?" my father called.

"Jammed up as far as you can see," said the man.

We waited. The sun shone hotly on the wrecked cars, on the scrubby hills running up from each side of the freeway. The man climbed down off his car.

"Where were you caught?" he asked my father.

"The stadium. Two out in the last of the seventh."

"Yeah, I was listening on the radio. Happened about twenty seconds later here."

"You cracked up, eh?"

"Yeah. The darkness partly, partly just the shock of looking down and seeing my bare knees."

He laughed. He was a paunchy, hairy man, balding. But he had a nice face.

"What do you think is happening?" my father asked.

"It's gotta be something from outer space," said the man. "That huge silver disk. I work at Douglas. Advanced space-vehicle design. We've got nothing like that. Neither have the Russians."

"And the language," my father said. "Did you hear that? It sounded like nothing I'd ever heard before."

The car ahead inched forward.

"I'm heading for Alhambra," said my father. "You want a lift?"

"Thanks. I'm just over the line in Pasadena."

The man got in. We inched forward. The sun beat down. Men and boys were working on their cars in their underwear or standing about on the roofs, looking out for tow trucks. A few women were waiting beside their cars in bathing suits, but all the way to Alhambra I only saw one woman in her underwear. She was beautiful, like Miss America, sunbathing on top of a Cadillac, her long blonde hair curling softly around her shoulder, her crimson toenails gleaming in the sunlight. A chauffeur had his head buried in the Cadillac's engine and a man with a little white mustache, a pot belly and skinny legs was stamping about impatiently in gold lamé underdrawers, puffing on a black cigar.

It took us three hours to get home. At first people yelled and cussed at each other out of their car windows; horns honked. We passed a couple of fights; cars clanked and bumped. The median was crowded with hurrying people; others were climbing over the freeway fences and running off down the streets or across the fields. But after a while, when people realized nothing else was going to happen right away, they calmed down. My father smoked his pipe and talked about power boats with the man we'd picked up. People joked about their underwear as we inched by stalled cars. Four men were sitting cross-legged on the roof of a VW microbus playing cards.

Still, everybody's voice, even joking, had an edge to it. People were still scared, dazed, wondering what had happened. All radios, TVs, and telephones had been knocked out. At first there'd been long lines by all the telephone booths we'd passed, but by now everybody'd given up; the booths were deserted; the freeway was littered with transistor radios.

So we inched along through the wrecks toward Alhambra. Occasionally a police helicopter would pass down the freeway, broadcasting appeals for calm. One reported that since the initial 'phenomenon' there had been no further hostile activity throughout the continental United States.

It was just that at 3:13 P.M. on August 10th all clothes other than underwear had suddenly vanished, leaving a faint smell of charred cloth and deodorant. Vanished from the stores, too, by the way — after we left the freeway, we passed the smouldering remains of a men's haberdashery and two or three boutiques. Through the windows of a supermarket I glimpsed still smoking clothing racks. Empty laundry baskets littered the streets outside the laundromats.

"Hey, Tim," said Joe, interrupting. "Hold on, Albert. Hey, Tim, here's seventy-five cents. Go across the street to Albrecht's and get us all a Popsicle. I want orange."

"Me, too."

"Grape."

"Lime."

"Wait till I get back, Albert," said Tim. He ran off. We lay sleepily in the shade of the Abraham Lincoln maple. A truck rattled by down Smith Street.

Tim came back and handed around the Popsicles.

"Ready?" said Albert, stripping the wrapper off his Popsicle with his teeth.

We nodded.

"Yeah."

"Shoot."

"Right."

My mother and Janie and the baby were home when we got there. They'd been shopping at the Safeway supermarket when it happened. Mom had opened a box of animal crackers for the baby and then set about making clothing for herself and Janie out of Scotch tape and cereal boxes. They'd arrived home dressed as Captain Crunch and the Cheerios' kid.

All evening we huddled together in the living room, waiting for whatever was going to happen. About ten my mother snuck out to the kitchen and made us all peanut butter sandwiches. At midnight, nine hours after the first attack, my father and mother decided it would be all right for us kids to go up to bed. My father started upstairs with the baby, Janie and me dragging sleepily behind . . .

lightning and thunder again!

In the kitchen my mother screamed. We all tumbled back downstairs. My mother was hugging herself in front of the open refrigerator, pointing at it with a ghastly expression. We crowded around the door and looked in. It was empty.

"It's empty," says my father. "What's the matter?"

"That's just it," croaked my mother. "A minute ago it was *full.*"

My father pushed the baby into my mother's arms and flung open the staples cabinet. Empty. The vegetable bin under the sink. Empty. Spice cabinet. Empty. He gazed distracted out the window at the branches of the eucalyptus tree nodding in the breeze under the street light. Then he dashed down to the cellar, three steps at a time. We heard the doors of my mother's canning shelves slamming open. Silence. Then, slowly: clump clump clump. My father came back upstairs and slumped down in a chair at the kitchen table.

"Empty," he said.

We all sat down around the kitchen table. Pretty soon the baby, who'd slept through most of it anyway, began to snore softly. Then Janie's head nodded and she slid slowly down in her chair, fast asleep.

I yawned and said, "I'm gonna shut my eyes to rest them but I'm not gonna sleep."

The next thing I knew morning sunlight was streaming through the curtains and our dog Heidi was scratching at the door to be let in. My mother was filling the kettle at the sink and yawning; the baby was kicking her feet in her cradle; my father was yawning and stretching in the doorway to the dining room; Janie was splashing water daintily on her eyes at the sink.

But the refrigerator door hung open, Captain Crunch still waved jauntily at me from my mother's back, and the baby began to scream

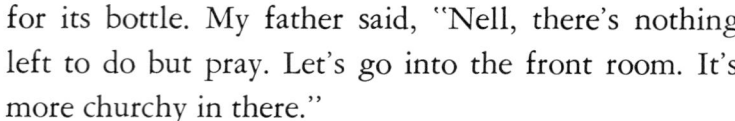

for its bottle. My father said, "Nell, there's nothing left to do but pray. Let's go into the front room. It's more churchy in there."

So we went into the front room and started to get down on our knees beside the rubber plant.

"Look," said Janie, pointing.

One of the side windows had been removed, and in its place there was a gray plywood panel with five candy-striped faucets mounted in it. Over the faucets a pink neon sign in a strange language blinked on and off around a large mail slot.

"Ha," said my father. He reached out gingerly and turned on one of the faucets. A white liquid gushed out, gurgling and foaming. He turned off the faucet and flicking up a drop of the white liquid on his finger, cautiously smelled and then tasted it.

"Milk." He tasted another drop. "Milk."

"Maybe it's poisoned, George."

"It tastes all right."

He thought a moment. Then,

"Albert. Let Heidi in and bring a saucer."

Heidi lapped it all up and barked for more. So we waited an hour, watching Heidi (who'd curled up and gone to sleep on the hearth rug), while Janie cleaned up the milk on the floor, and first my mother and then my father and finally me took turns walking and rocking and bouncing the screaming baby.

"Okay," said my father. "Let's eat."

Later, while the rest of us were dozing on the couches, my father deciphered the message above the faucets. It said we all had to do calisthenics every morning: Walter Camp's "Daily Dozen."

"Walter Camp's 'Daily Dozen'"? said my father. "Nobody's done that for forty years."

"It can't be a joke, George. Our clothes *did* vanish. And all our food."

Janie and I were playing checkers on the floor. My father was reading last night's paper. My mother was sewing Janie a robe out of the dining room curtains.

"But they can't be *serious*. Walter Camp's 'Daily Dozen'? They must be mad. Our clothes and food vanish; the whole stadium, 50,000 people, are stripped to their underwear, and the only instructions are to do Walter Camp's 'Daily Dozen' every morning?"

Steve got up, brushing the grass off the seat of his pants.

"I got to go. My Mom said I had to watch the baby while she went to the store."

We watched him trudging off up the street through the wavy heat. At least Albert and Joe and I did. Tim had gone to sleep under his pith helmet.

"Okay," I said when Steve had turned out of sight up Cherry Street.

"Where was I?" said Albert.

"The calisthenics."

"Oh. Yeah. Well . . ."

"Is it much longer?" asked Joe.

"Naw. Five, six minutes."

"Okay. Because I got to go pretty soon, too. I gotta be there when my father gets home from work. We're going fishing up to Sprout Lake."

"Well," said Albert.

So the next morning my father said, "Humph, *he* wasn't going to do any calisthenics." And the second he said it

BLAM!

a pink plastic arm as big as Raquel Welch's hip came crashing through the side of the house and cuffed him on the back so he sprawled across the couch. And then a huge voice boomed:

"Corbalisthenics!"

My father jumped up, torn shirt, wrenched aching back and all, and calisthenicked frantically, like a man in an old movie, till the voice boomed:

"Orbenough! "Torbake orbout yorbour borbooks. "Torburn torbo porbage orbone. Morbemorize sorbections orbone throrbough forbive."
The huge fist pounded the floor.

"Yorbou horbave tworbenty-tworbo morbinutes torbo corbomplete yorbour worbork. Storbart!"
Four workbooks tumbled through the mail slot. My father and Janie and me set to work, scared stiff. My mother was tucking the baby into her crib.

"Orball!"
booms the voice and the mammoth arm floated farther in through the splintered wall and pinched my mother cruelly through her boxtop.

"Orball!"
So my mother ran and snatched up her workbook and we all studied violently, groaning with fear, glancing every few seconds behind us to make sure the fist was still floating over the couch, not sneaking through the lamps and endtables toward us.

All day, textbooks, workbooks, quizzes, dittoed worksheets tumbled, slid and slithered through the mail slot: first, "lorbanguage orband lorbiterature," then, "morbath," then, "sorbocial storbudies," then, "gorbeography" — all day long, from eight-thirty in the morning till four-thirty in the afternoon — except for once in the morning and once in the afternoon when the voice boomed:

RORBECESS!

And we were so relieved to have the pressure off us for a few minutes, we felt so free, bursting, all the fear and boredom and frustration of the lessons fountaining up out of us, that all of us, my father and mother, too, ran around and around the living room. We leaped over the footstools, clambered over the couch — my father vaulted an armchair — waving our arms, shouting madly, till the voice boomed:

CLORBASSTIME!

and the pink plastic fist rose up from behind the love seat, where it had been smoking a cigarette through a hole in its palm, and tinkled a tiny Tibetan temple bell. We plunged back to studying.

At noon we slurped up our milk hurriedly, silently. Once my father started to whisper something over the edge of his glass to my mother, but the voice boomed:

"Sorbilence! Orbeat! Norbo torbalking! Morbillions orbof orbothers orbare worbaiting forbor yorbou torbo forbinish sorbo thorbey corban orbeat."

After we'd finished, the fist disappeared out the hole in the wall, and while Janie and I played checkers, my father and mother frantically bottled and changed the baby. Fifteen minutes later the fist plunged in through the wall again and herded us with its monstrous prodding forefinger back to our workbooks. At four-thirty it thundered:

"Schorbools orbout! Horbomework!" and disappeared as thick stacks of dittoed "morbultiple chorboice" and "trorbue orbor forbalse" worksheets slid through the mail slot.

Janie and I did them right away and *then* played because we knew how it was with homework, but my father said he'd do his later and went over to talk the whole thing over with Mr. Carstairs, who lives next door. He was still working on his papers at eight-thirty when the lights went out and the voice boomed:

BORBEDTIME!

He tried to finish under the covers with a flashlight, but the mammoth fist caught him at it, stripping the covers back, pinching and poking him. So next morning when the voice boomed:

PORBASS ORBIN YORBOUR HORBOMEWORK

he was only about half done and had to stay behind in the living room that afternoon and write, "Orbi worbill corbomplete morby horbomework orbeveryday" five hundred times.

After the first few days of Orb rule, by the time the strangeness had worn off, Janie and me and most of the other kids in the neighborhood had settled in pretty well. We were used to fitting into a system like the Orb's. I was in the sixth grade, after all, and Janie the fourth. But a lot of the grownups cracked. One day during "morbath" (everybody ran on the same schedule, which made it hard for those who had babies or old people to take care of or were used to afternoon naps), anyway, one day during "morbath" Mr. Carstairs ran out of his house, tearing off his undershirt, and shinnied up a palm tree. He perched up there all that day and the next night, singing silly songs and sticking out his tongue at the two fists which were guarding the bottom of the tree. But the next day at noon he slid down, hanging his head, and scuffed, pale and drawn and unshaven, up the front walk onto his porch, took his pinching and went back to his workbook. Other grownups who couldn't fit in — for instance, those who kept asking the fists questions or talking during lessons — were shipped off to special "dorbisciplinary" schools or "prorbisons" where they were locked away with hardened "orbunder orbachievers." Hardly any of them returned *better* — I mean, they were usually *more* obstreperous and rebellious than before. But I guess the Orbs didn't care; they'd just spirit them away again — almost any evening you could go up on the roof and see the golden twilight sky seething with fists carrying away "morbisfits."

Of course, the grownups had a lot harder time learning the Orb subjects, too, because, well, take for instance, "morbath." Before the Orbs came, $2 + 2 = 4$, right? Well, the Orbs said, "Norbo, wrorbong. $4 + 4 = 2$." So someone like my father had to *un*learn $2 + 2 = 4$ before he could *learn* $4 + 4 = 2$."

"Then what would $2 + 2$ equal?" asked Joe.
"One," said Albert.
"Yeah. And $1 + 1$?"
"Zero."
"You mean, zorbero," I said.
"Yeah. Zorbero."
"Well, then, what's 35 divided by 5?" said Joe.
Albert thought a moment: "175 and a few cents extra."
"How about 16 *multiplied* by 12?" I said.
"Hey, look," said Albert, "you want to hear the rest of the story or you want to mess around with a lot of stupid stuff like that?"
"*16 multiplied by 12.*"

"Ah . . . one and one-third. Okay."

I thought a moment. "Okay."

"So it was harder for the grownups in that way, too. But us kids, we didn't care. We'd have had to be going to school, learning something, even if the Martians hadn't come, and it didn't make much difference whether it was $2 + 2 = 4$ or $4 + 4 = 2$, whether it was 'The Persians Lost the Battle of Salamis' or 'Thorbe Porbersians Lorbost thorbe Borbattle orbof Sorbalamis.' It was all the same to us. We still had to break our heads studying. Just like before."

"So what finally happened?" said Joe. "I got to go."

"Nothing," said Albert. "There was no way to get rid of the Orbs. As their planet shriveled and peeled in space like an onion, more and more of them came. You could hardly ever get a seat on a bus anymore. There were always long lines at the checkout counters in the department stores."

"But after everybody'd gotten used to the new system, they found they could endure it. Of course, lots dropped out, went bad, ended up in 'prorbison.' But that happens anyway. You got to expect a lot of rejects with *any* system. Most people gradually settled in, like someone hitching about to get comfortable in a lumpy armchair. There were no clothes, of course. The Orbs always insisted on that. But people let their hair grow down to their waists and wore strings and strings of beads. My father and I'd go out to Anaheim to watch the Mets and Dodgers play, just like we had that first day, and there'd be Tom Seaver out on the mound in blue undershorts with an orange stripe across the seat (the Mets' colors, you know) and his hair down to his waist, writhing up in the wind every time he pitched. And fifty thousand people enjoying the warm sun in their underwear, their hair wrapped around their arms out of the way, or sticking up all over their heads so they looked like hedgehogs. Then Seaver would strike out the side and the crowd would rise, roaring, their hairy arms and chests shining in the sunlight. Oh, it was a grand sight!

"Most people learned 'morbath' and 'lorbiterature' and 'gorbeography,' and after they'd received their 'dorbiplomas,' went out to work for the Orbs in one of the factories manufacturing 'norbeon horbot dorbogs' or 'glorbass brorbead' or 'vorbegetable sorboup.' Or they worked on the great 'sorbeaweed' plantations or 'orbonion' farms. Kids still played hide-and-seek and kick-the-can in backyards and vacant lots, coming in for supper with burrs and potato bugs in their long hair, their undershorts splattered with mud. Fathers still strolled home from the bus stop in the dusk, calling hello to their neighbors, loosening their daffodil-leaf neckties. Everything was about the same as it had always been. Only instead of your mother or father grabbing you by the collar and wrenching you out from behind the furnace where you and Bill Sturts had been looking through your father's copy of *Plorbayboy, Morbale* or the special Norbative Trorbibes issue of the *Norbational Gorbeographic,* it was a mammoth, pimply, pink-plastic fist. So who cared? You got yanked. And then pinched. *Caught.* That was what mattered."

Albert yawned and stretched.

"Finished?" asked Joe.

He nodded.

"Pretty good," I said. "Pretty good. Tell your father he did all right."

"Aw, I don't know," said Joe. "All that stuff about underwear. Who's interested in underwear?"

I reached over and rumpled Tim's shoulder to wake him. His face was all hot and sweaty and creased under the pith helmet. He looked dazed.

"C'mon," said Joe. "I got to go."

"So go on then."

"Naw, come with me. If my father's not home yet, I'm liable to get hooked into something by my sisters unless you come. Wait with me. C'mon, I bought you all Popsicles, didn't I?"

(See *Hot IV*, page 124)

JAAAAAACK MEARS!
A CAUTIONARY TALE

I.
>
> January's
> necessary.
I knew a boy forgot it once —
and February, March, April, May,
>   and twenty-one days in June —
but not his lunchpail —
>   dug all day
> on the town dump,
tugging and heaving on boards
to uncover boxes of unknown
>   junk:
>   Cologne
bottles, a Gramophone,
>   banging and prying
>   in its innards.

>   Tuesday,
where the river leaped and bucked
> under the bridge,
> icing bouldery abutments,
then slid out black and sinuous
>   between snowy banks,
>   he broke ice
>   with an alder pole
and tramped as far as the ruined mill,
>   where he could hear the hogs
>   grunting
>   in the pens at Sharkey's.

              Wednesday,
      hunting chipmunks
in a stone wall crumbling across Red Mountain,
              he came,
through woods and a snowy, overgrown field,
               at dusk,
      to a deserted house.

            Thursday,
      setting out
with lunchpail and his father's flashlight
        from the kitchen . . .
his mother called to him
      from the hall telephone.

              "Sit down."
"I got . . ."
              "Sit down."

      Hitching up his pants
      to the clonk of the teakettle
      on the front burner.

                    "Now.
Why weren't you in school
                this week?"

"In summer, Ma?"

              "It   is   the   5th   of   January
              YOUNG MAN!
                    Summer!?!"

"Ma, it *isn't*!
  it's *June*.
    School closed last Friday,
        June 19th."

"JAAAAAACK MEEEEEEARS!
don'tyoutrytotellmeyouthinkit's   JUNE!"
   "It is, Ma.   Look.
      Haven't
         I got my summer pants on?
      Haven't
         I put my skis and skates
         away in the attic?"

   "Jack Mears, I'll tan your hide for this.
      You get to school
                        NOW!"

"Ma, it's all shut up. Ma look,
   I got my sneakers on,
                  a towel,
      my bathing suit under my pants.
      See?
We're going swimming, me and Billy,
but you don't have to worry, Ma,
         his brother's coming.
         He says he'll watch us."
                              "Hand them to me."
"Ma . . ."
"Now go to school,
                  young man,
anddon'tletmehearanyofthisfoolishnessagain."

II.

His mother sniffled,
         peeling onions at the sink.
Hanging up his hat on the closet door:
         "Ma, I did what you said.
                              NOW
         can I go swimming?"

III.

"Agnes, he *must* be teasing you. He couldn't actually *believe*
        it's June.
There's a foot of snow on the ground."

"He couldn't keep it up this long, Tom, if he didn't.
    Everytime I speak to him
        he agrees with me,
running fawningly to do whatever I've asked
      as if he's humoring me,
        as if it was *me* that was crazy."
      She shut the icebox.

    "He came downstairs after school
        with his baseball uniform on,
          whistling
        and pounding his glove."

"Did he go to school?"

    "I was too ashamed to call and check."

His father rinsed his cup at the sink.
    "I'll stay home
        tomorrow."

IV.

Under the sullen bank of clouds in the east
        dawn leaked cold and white.

"Ma. Ma, somebody took my blankets."

    "I put them away for the summer, Jack."
Gray light seeped into his room,
        glinting on piles of toys,
    his posters, electric-train tracks.

He climbed shivering out of bed.
   The floor was as cold as a dungeon.
      Hopping,
        he pulled his baseball shirt
        over his goose-pimpled arms.

   "Ready, Jack?"
His father clumped into the kitchen in waders.
    "They won't bite after the sun's up.
      Better hurry."
"I thought I'd have some cocoa, Pop."
    Hunched up beside the icebox,
       rubbing his cold hands.
"COCOA!   In June?"
     Smash on the back.
   "Toughen up, Jack. Let's go."

v.

Clambering down the slippery boulders,
   the snowstorm swirling around him,
soft flakes vanishing
     in the plunging water curling
     over on its brown back . . .

   For years and years
    he huddled
  over his hunched-up knees,
    trembling,   sleepy,
    the rod bobbing in the wind and snow.

His father knocked out his pipe on an icy boulder.
   "Guess we'll have to come back
           tomorrow."

VI.

    The kitchen curtains billowed
        in the wind.
"Hi Jack. No luck?"
        He shook his head, shoving away his rod
and creel in the closet,
                his fingers
    like raw carrots.

VII.

"Now go outside and play."
    Hugging himself,
        scrounged into a corner
        out of the January wind,
    he gritted his teeth.

VIII.

    His father shook out his newspaper.
    His mother took dishes of coldcuts and potato salad
        out of the icebox.

    He squinted through his glass of water,
                                then:
"Did the Yankees win today, Pop?"

        Silence.

    The faucet dripping into the sink.
  A gust of wind rattled the stormdoor.
"Did they?"
        "Seven
                to
                      three."

IX.

The bowl of Wheaties and peaches melted from his fingers,
    shattering
        on the flagstones.
    Milk dripped
        from the cuffs of his Levi's,
peaches grinned up from his sneakers.
    "*SUMMER*
        school?"
"Yes, your mother and I have decided."

X.

    The kitchen door banged.
      "MA? I'M HOME!"
    He rummaged in the kitchen closet among the overshoes.
    "Billy and me are going over to Kelly's to play ball."
His mother came slowly up the cellar stairs
    and set the laundry basket on the table.
    "Jack, what are you doing home so early?"
Crawling deeper into the closet behind the hanging overcoats,
    over tennis rackets,
        outgrown overshoes,
    "Didn't you hear the fire trucks go by?"
        "What fire trucks?"
                "The school burned down, Ma.
                Summer school's canceled.
                Mr. Gross said in assembly
                    we may not
                    even have school
                      next
              SEPTEMBER."

Entomological Soup

1 soup bone	2 lbs. potatoes
1 parsnip	5 hairy centipedes
4 carrots	1 head cabbage
3 small onions	8 black beetles
6 hellgrammites	7 pismires
3 termites	15 green beetles
1 bunch celery	salt and pepper

Bring 2 quarts of dishwater to a boil, add the soup bone, insects, parsnip, cabbage (shredded), carrots, onions, celery (chopped), and whole peeled potatoes. Simmer for 1 hour, then strain. Pick the insect corpses out of the vegetables and chop fine, setting one pismire, one green bettle, and two centipedes aside on a saucer. Return the vegetables and chopped insects to the broth, heat, and serve with crackers or buttered toast. When someone asks, "What kind of soup is this, dear?" go to the kitchen — ostensibly to look up the name of the soup in the cookbook — and return with the saucer on which are drying the water-logged corpses of the pismire, the green beetle, and the two centipedes.

* *Special hints to careful cooks:* Do not return from the kitchen until everybody at the table has finished at least half his soup.

Lay the saucer in the center of the table and crow:
"Entomological Soup!"

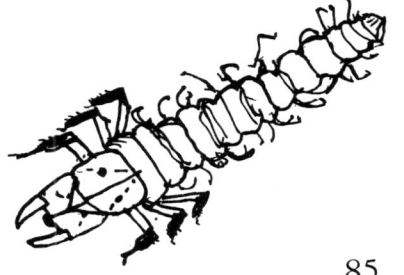

Your brother will sneer and ask, "What's that?" (Your parents will either continue to eat, chatting among themselves, or grab you. Be prepared.)

Thrust the saucer under your brother's ugly nose, crow, "BUG soup, smarty pants!" and run.

This dish is especially effective when served to a brother who has tormented his sister and her girl friends with spiders and centipedes dangling on threads.

A note on ingredients: Other insects may be substituted for those listed without detracting from the effectiveness of the soup. Note, however, that spiders shrivel when boiled, unless extremely large and hairy (in which case they may be poisonous; use caution in capturing; one does not want to have to throw out the cook with the soup). Thus, to get an effect of insect feet and legs in your soup, centipedes are preferable. Do not use fleas except in extreme cases, for they are carriers of bubonic plague.

* *Special hints number 2:* Before serving this soup, a careful cook will store a week or ten days' supply of canned goods and crackers under the shoes in his bedroom closet, for it is unwise to accept food cooked or served by others until the éclat of your soup has worn away.

Diverted Haddock

Have at room temperature a 2-lb. haddock, whole, gutted, and scraped.

Combine: *2 tablespoons soft butter, ¼ teaspoon pepper or paprika, a fresh grating of nutmeg.*

Rub the haddock all over with this, then place him (or her — it is difficult to tell with haddock) in an ovenproof dish. Cover with a close-fitting lid. Bake in a moderate oven (350°) until tender.

Then make a small cut under a bone in the haddock's stomach and insert a printed slip bearing the words: "This Van Heusen shirt inspected by number 44268" or "Factory warranted for normal use up to ninety days. Call J. C. Ward, 32 LaCienega Boulevard, Los Angeles, California 90212."

Melt: *4 tablespoons butter.*

Add: *½ cup dry white wine, juice of ½ lemon, 2 tablespoons chopped parsley.*

Heat the sauce well but do not permit it to boil. Pour this over the haddock and serve garnished with parsley.

While your parents and older brothers and sisters are excitedly discussing how the printed slips came to be in the haddock's stomach, *divert* your portion of haddock into a small plastic bag in your lap. Place the plastic bag in the pocket of your dress and talking as if your mouth is full, join the discussion.

Special hints to careful cooks: Such comments as "Gosh, I thought haddock tasted like *fish*!" or "Gee, Mom, I certainly can cook fish!" may prove helpful.

Boiled Kvetch

10 *loaves of unsliced Wonder Bread*
16 *dispensers of 1-inch Scotch tape*
2 *one-pound balls of twine*
3 *quarts of piccalilli*
3 *quarts of used sauerkraut*
1 *bottle of Heinz Ketchup*
2 *jars of mustard*
10 *Hershey bars with almonds*
1 *kvetch or small nagging sister*

Slice the ten loaves of bread thickly, spread the slices out on the floor, and tape securely together so that a long, thick blanket of Wonder Bread is formed.

Shake the kvetch, holding her upside down by the heels, until silent and red-faced. Then lay her on her back on the blanket of Wonder Bread and tie it around her, folding the edges in so that a broad opening runs along the top.

Mix in a large bowl the 3 quarts of piccalilli, 1 quart of the used sauerkraut, and the bottle of Heinz Ketchup. Add any crumbs and scraps of tape which may be scattered about the floor. Apply this paste with a large spoon to the kvetch. Special care should be taken to work it into her hair.

The rest of the used sauerkraut may then be sprinkled slowly on with a cooking fork. If the kraut has dried while in the icebox, add water in which four orange peels, a sliced plum, one cup of vanilla ice cream, and two old sneakers have been soaked overnight. The mustard, which should be cold, may be applied with a spatula about the cheeks and chin. Garnish with Hershey bars.

* *Special hints to careful cooks:* Should the kvetch or small nagging sister object at any point, threaten to summon the McElroys' dog, assuring her that its favorite meal is a screeching frankfurter with all the trimmings.

Serving suggestions: Boiled kvetch must be eaten by at least five children, who should approach it horribly, brandishing carving knives and forks and gnashing their teeth. Cries of "Thigh! Thigh!" "Oh, them toes is succulent!" "Don't pig the nose, Jane!" and "Ear! Ear!" will enhance the general effect. Monstrous sucking and chewing noises should accompany the eating of the Hershey bars.

* *Special hints number 2:* Save two Hershey bars for the kvetch to eat when she arises from her bed of bread. Otherwise, that night at dinner, instead of something pleasant like ice cream or pie, you may receive your *just* dessert.

Liver Punishment
For parents who make their children eat liver.

Tell your mother you will cook dinner and then purchase the following:

4 TV dinners (roast turkey with bullet peas is best because worst, but individual preferences should be taken into account. For instance, if your father is particularly fond of roast beef, the roast beef TV dinner will cause him more unhappiness than any other.)

4 tart shells
1 quart lemon jello
2 cups bittersweet chocolate sauce

Place the TV dinners in the oven and cook according to the directions on the boxes. Then turn the oven down to 200° and permit the TV dinners to desiccate for 33 minutes. When the peas have shriveled, the sliced turkey turned tan, curling up at the edges, and a scum has formed on the mashed potatoes and gravy, garnish with paprika and moldy parsley and serve.

Place the four tart shells on a cookie tin and burn until black. Cool and then stuff with lemon jello. Bathe in bittersweet chocolate sauce, sprinkle generously with floor sweepings, and serve.

Special hints to careful cooks: Set the table as if for a party — your mother's best linen napkins and silverware, candles, fresh flowers — and keep asking your parents anxiously how they like your dinner: "Is it all right, Daddy? Is it? Really?" In this way your dinner will become a special occasion in your parents' minds, and they will be too kind-hearted to suggest Schrafft's, or even the Automat, instead.

You must also include a TV dinner for yourself. Otherwise your parents, realizing suddenly that you are serving Liver Punishment, will mandate Schrafft's but leave you home to eat cold milktoast in the kitchen while the babysitter reads her newspaper and sucks a toothpick.

Fruit Kiss
A Simple but Effective Dessert

Peel a large orange. Divide and skin several sections carefully while eating the rest. Place the skinned sections in a plastic bag in the pocket of your dress or shirt. When you see your uncle's car lurch over the corner of the curb into the driveway, place one skinned section in your mouth. Do not chew. Stand in the open doorway, waving. When your aunt bends down to kiss you, tongue the juicy orange section out between your lips so that she kisses that.

If, while greeting your parents, she offers you her bristly cheek to kiss, take another juicy orange section out of the plastic bag and poke it into her ear.

Parent's Goose

*Recommended for the parent
who calls his child names
or spanks him
in front of his friends.*

To cook a Parent's Goose, place in a bowl: *½ cup lard*

Pour over it: *¼ cup boiling water*

Beat these ingredients until they are cold and creamy.

Sift *1½ cups cake flour, ½ teaspoon baking powder, ½ teaspoon salt.*

Combine the liquid and the sifted ingredients and stir them until they form a smooth ball. Cover the dough and chill until firm. Roll it, place the top and bottom crusts in separate pans, and bake at 450° for 15 minutes or until brown. While the crust is cooling on the windowsill, write on small slips of white cardboard all of your parent's bad habits or unfortunate failings that you can remember. For instance, a father may leave his pajamas in a heap on the bathroom floor every morning or forget to put the top back on the toothpaste. His socks may smell; he may suck his teeth after eating corn on the cob at home or argue in a loud voice with your mother in restaurants.

A mother may snore or talk all morning on the telephone. She may borrow towels from resort hotels, chew gum while cleaning house with her hair in

rollers, cheat on the grocery bill at the supermarket, or do ugly exercises to television after your father has left for work in the morning.

Place the slips of cardboard in the pie, glue the top crust on with Elmer's glue, and serve as a surprise at your parents' next formal dinner party.

Fried Hall Closet

*A dish for parents who have refused
to take a child to the circus.*

To prepare, boil six pairs of your mother's old shoes till gooey. Cool; add one quart of trampled hats, four right-hand gloves, one rubber (minced), a tablespoon of sugar, and two cloves.

Fry gently in a silver bowl until crisp (silver bowls are usually found wrapped in tissue paper in a dining room cupboard). Garnish with a selection of your father's ties, and place on the hall table so that it will be discovered by your parents on their return, laughing and talking, from the movies.

Soiled Eggs

A Picnic Dish

Hardboil four eggs, wrap in waxed paper, and insert carefully in a paper bag with your sandwiches and an orange.

At noon, when the teacher or counselor calls everyone to lunch at the benched tables under the trees, do not pause. Run perspiring and breathless to your paper bag. DO NOT WASH YOUR HANDS. Crack an egg on a friend's head and peel it. Then toss it gently from grimy hand to grimy hand, now and again squeezing it so the skin splits and the yolk leers yellowly up through the white.

Offer the egg to any teachers or grownups who might be along or to fastidious girls (those, for instance, who have spent the morning sitting on the benches talking and giggling, surreptitiously eyeing the eighth-grade boys).

Candied Peach

Melt: *4½ teaspoons butter*
Add: *1½ cups molasses, ¾ cup sugar*
Stir until the sugar is dissolved and then boil without stirring until viscous and sticky.

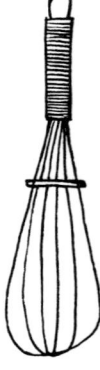

During recess paint this syrup on the Peach's desk and chair so that when she comes running in, pink-cheeked, bright-eyed and laughing, and pauses to pout and stick out her tongue and laugh at you, and then, flouncing up her long, auburn hair, bounces down into her chair ... she'll feel a cold and gluey wetness ... and start back, frightened, her eyes widening, and stick to the back of the seat and scream, and slamming her dainty white hands on the desk, try to push herself up, and stick, and begin to cry, laying her head helplessly on the desk, and stick, and try to kick the desk away, and stick! stick! stick! stick! And serve her right for teasing, miserable pretty girl.

Infested Spinach

To one package of frozen leaf spinach add a dead mouse. Serve silently in a large dish. When the mouse is discovered, screech and tremble. Recovered, comment: "Gosh! Mrs. Witherpoop, our science teacher, *told* us all the spinach was infested with mice this year, but, gee, I thought she only meant the *fresh* spinach." Later, over dessert, remark: "I don't think I could ever eat spinach again, Dad, do you?"

A note on ingredients: A dead mouse may usually be obtained by trading at school. The current values (as of March 17, 1974, at Overlook School, La-Grangeville, New York) are:

> house mouse: a doll's arm, a jackknife with broken blade, and a slightly used but not linty lime lollipop.
> meadow mouse: a blank report card, a plastic Abraham-Lincoln-head-pencil-sharpener, and a jackknife which has been used to cut wire and stab tin cans.
> (*Prices slightly higher west of the Mississippi*)

Special hints to careful cooks: The use of a dead rat is not recommended, since the discovery of such a gross, garbage-eating, flea-infested animal may cause so much commotion and distress that your later comments will not be attended to. In addition, it is extremely unlikely, except in large families, that there will be sufficient spinach to properly conceal a rat.

Brother's Hash

To settle a brother's hash, boil his tennis hat for fifteen minutes. Hang in the pantry to cool.

Then lay his four favorite comic books on the kitchen table and spread mustard on page 14 of the first, page 19 of the second, page 28 of the third, and page 35 of the fourth. While the mustard is drying, cut the erasers off all his pencils, place in an ovenproof dish, garnish with his rawhide bootlaces, and bake slowly in a moderate oven until brown.

Place in the cooled but sodden tennis hat, the following:

> *his jackknife*
> *one of the casters from his bed*
> *his rattlesnake skin*
> *his arrowheads*
> *his World War I ammunition pouch*
> *the key to his tin cashbox*
> *the autographed baseball he borrowed from Joe Anders*

Stir in the baked erasers and rawhide laces. Set on the window sill to solidify.

Then fry his new sneakers in salad oil until crisp, pour two tablespoons of maple syrup into the toes of his hiking boots, and drop his baseball cards into one quart of lukewarm water to soak. While the cards are melting, eat a slice of cake, guzzle a Coca-Cola, and, stuffing your pockets with nuts and oranges, climb to the top of the maple tree in the backyard. Do not come down until late that night after the whole family, wandering through the fields with flashlights, calling and searching, has become frantic, and your brother, standing under the tree beside your mother (who is sniveling into her apron), says, "Gee, if he'd only come back, I wouldn't even be mad at him for what he did." Then rumple your hair, rip your shirttail, roll up one trouser leg, smudge your cheeks with crumbled bark, and clamber clumsily down.

Additional Recipes

which may be obtained by writing the publishers
(letters must be postmarked after June 10, 1984)

Repelling Shad	*Plucked Goose*	*Sautéed Oldsmobile*
Cheesed Head	*Fresh Tongue*	(this will require a very large pan)
Pickled Mother	*Apple Surprise*	*Substituted Pastry*

Drawings by Abigail and Barnaby

Yrots A

Well, see . . . I mean . . . Look . . .

This like was it. Town in children the all for party tea June Forsythe's Mrs. to sister my behind along trailing was I. Cripes! It to go to wanted who? Me not. Scone a each us gave butler the while lemonade pouring mansion her of porch the on there sat she.

"Dear, year this you are how? One just, no, no." Show puppet stupid a be would there maybe and lawn the on around stand go all we'd then and. Magician dumb a or. Sake cripes for, us to poems recited she'd; anything had hadn't she year one. Was it which, shade the in hundred nine was it if even coat a and tie a and shirt white a wear to had you and.

Hill the up sister my behind along sweating and itchy trailed I so. It loved she . . .

Aw, that's no good. Telling it in backward sentences is just as dull dull dull, dull
       dull
       dull

   dull
dull *dull*

llud llud llud

as writing forwards. Besides, she'd flunk me sure, and then there'd be a d u l l   d u l l e r   DULL- EST! lecture from my father to listen to.

Maaaaaaaaaaaaaaayy 27th. Eight days to go.
E   I   G   H   T
8:45 to 3:15 = six and one-half hours. Less an hour for lunch and goofing off in study hall. Times eight = forty-four hours. Or, lemme see, two thousand six hundred and forty minutes. I can't stand it.

She's eyeing me. If I don't get this composition done, it'll be two thousand six hundred and eighty-five minutes, because she'll keep me after school.

I GOT IT! How could she complain? Tell a story she said. Okay. Here goes:

5

The End.

So we trudged home hungry, combing mouse turds and dust and oatmeal out of our hair, while Alice revived Mrs. Forsythe with cold compresses, and the butler, groaning, staggered off to his room. We didn't even get a scone. And she'd planned a special treat: hot dogs.

It *was* ketchup. All day that dog had crouched on the top shelf waiting for Silas to wander in. When Mrs. Forsythe had opened the cabinet, Silas rubbing up against her leg and purring, the butler waiting behind her with a tray, the dog had bolted out in a shower of canned goods, knocking Mrs. Forsythe and the butler over. Silas had leapt up a window curtain, in and out of a cabinet, caterwauling, the dog yapping-galloping after him, scrabbling over dishes, tin cans, in and out of another cabinet, back and forth over Mrs. Forsythe and the butler. A crock of marmalade had toppled onto Mrs. Forsythe's head, a five-pound can of honey onto the butler's.

Or was it ketchup?
Blood!?!

4

The butler lay unconscious in a corner. Mrs. Forsythe sprawled in the china cabinet, her head among the dangling teacups, her tongue hanging out, her white old-lady's hair red and gooey. Clouds of flour dust choked the air. Molasses oozed down one wall. Karo syrup glistened on another. Tins of nutmeg, Wheaties, rice, tea bags, Band Aids, chickpeas, oatmeal had disgorged their contents down the shelves, across the floor.

An unparalleled holocaust greeted our eyes.

Suddenly Silas Wilks, Mrs. Forsythe's old gray tomcat, shot between Alice's legs; she stumbled, grabbing the door. The door swung, dragging her down. A dog plunged by, spinning her topsy-turvey. The shotgun exploded into the ceiling; plaster and laths, beetle carcases and mouse turds rained down on our heads.

"Okay?" hissed Alice over her shoulder, easing open the door, clutching the shotgun.

"Oh. Oh. Oh. Oh. Oh."

Groans, *blood-curdling groans.*

"Come out!" she yelled again, brandishing the shotgun fiercely at the pantry door.

No answer.

"Come out with your hands up!" yelled Alice.

"Shhhh. Listen."

"What is it?"

Dick Bentley began to cry; Alice turned pale; some kids in the back screamed.

"What could it be?"

A rattling-clattling-growling-meowling rumpus was coming from the pantry.

"Listen!"

"Because that's where they *always* bury the body," said Alice. "I know. I've read up. Come on."

We crept through the kitchen.

3

"But why would he bury her in her own cellar where someone's sure to look?"

"Down cellar," said Alice.

"Where?"

"And he's buried her right in this house, too."

"It just looks like melted raspberry sherbet to me," somone muttered.

Alice pointed and gasped.

"And so then he says (mark my words, I've read up), he says, 'I'll have that diamond ring off yer finger, Mrs. Forsythe, my dear, if I have to kill you for it and *cut* it off, finger and all.' Look at that blood on the linoleum!"

"What'd he do then, Alice?"

"Gosh!"

"He leaped out from behind the icebox at her, grinning evilly so his gums showed just like when he's slicing bread. She was struck all of a heap, and tried to escape, whimpering. Look at the marks of her shoes there."

"You mean he *attacked* her?"

"Arrrrgh!" Alice pointed down the dim entryway into the kitchen, her gnarled old finger trembling. "It's John, the butler, boys and girls. Ain't it always the butler? Don't tell me, I've read up."

"*Who*, Alice?"

"Then someone's done away with her. I can smell it. Oh, poor Mrs. Forsythe."

"Sally and me looked in the garage, Alice."

"Me neither."

"No."

"Did you, too, Joe? You got the sharpest eyes."

"Yes."

"Did someone search the attic?"

"No, I didn't."

"No one found her? Al? Janie?"

2

Sam shook his head.
"Did you find her?"
"Yes?"
"Sam?"
"No."
"Irving?"
"Janet and I couldn't find her."
We gathered around Alice in the dining room, panting, jostling. Running through the mansion, we rummaged in closets and bureau drawers, peered under beds, climbed on chairs to look into the tops of cupboards. Alice paced back and forth on the great Aubusson carpet which stretched from the library to the dining room. She shook her head and rubbed her chin ominously, loading the double-barreled shotgun as she walked.

"Run!" she cried suddenly. "Run, children, I ain't seen hide nor hair of her since two myself. She may have fallen. Search the house. I'll fetch the old shotgun down from the mantelpiece in case there's been foul play."

Alice sucked the end of a knife.
"No."
"She ain't outside?" asked Alice.
"The cream in the silver pitcher has scum on it even. Susie poked her finger into it."
"The party was supposed to start at two, Alice. Do you know where Mrs. Forsythe is?"
Alice was polishing the silver in the dining room, humming quietly to herself.
"Let's go find Alice," said Tom. "She'll know where Mrs. Forsythe is. She's worked for her for thirty years almost."
"The teapot's cold."
"Nobody's here."
"Is it over already?" I chimed in.
"Hi Betty. Why's everybody just standing around?" called my sister.

1

We came out of the lilacs onto the driveway. All the kids were standing around on the porch of Mrs. Forsythe's mansion under the pillars. But Mrs. Forsythe's chair behind the silver samovar full of root beer was empty, and beside the plates of scones and a huge dish of hot dog rolls, where the butler usually stood, there was nobody.

"Yes," she said.

"Would you really tell Mom if I didn't go to the party?" I yelled ahead to my sister as we ducked through the lilacs at the edge of Mrs. Forsythe's driveway.

MRS. FORSYTHE'S PARTY

There. Let her try to figure that out. Hold it.

Check.

Check.
Check.

Check.

Okay. Checked and double-checked. Punctuation, spelling; it's got a beginning, a middle, and an end. Even if the end is the beginning and the beginning the end, and the beginning of the middle is really the end while the end's the beginning, but at least the middle of the middle's where it should be. If she says she doesn't understand it, I'll say, Huh! you call yourself a teacher?

Maybe that's too strong. I'll say, Huh! There's more than one way to skin a cat, you're reading it wrong, backwards, sdrawkcab, *look at the page numbers. You started on page 5, where it says The End. Try beginning on page 1, after the title. Ha. She'll either give me an A or cream me.*

Here goes.

Miss Meacham?

BIG BONUS GAME SECTION

Answers for the following quizzes are found on page 129.

CAN YOU DO THIS REBUS?

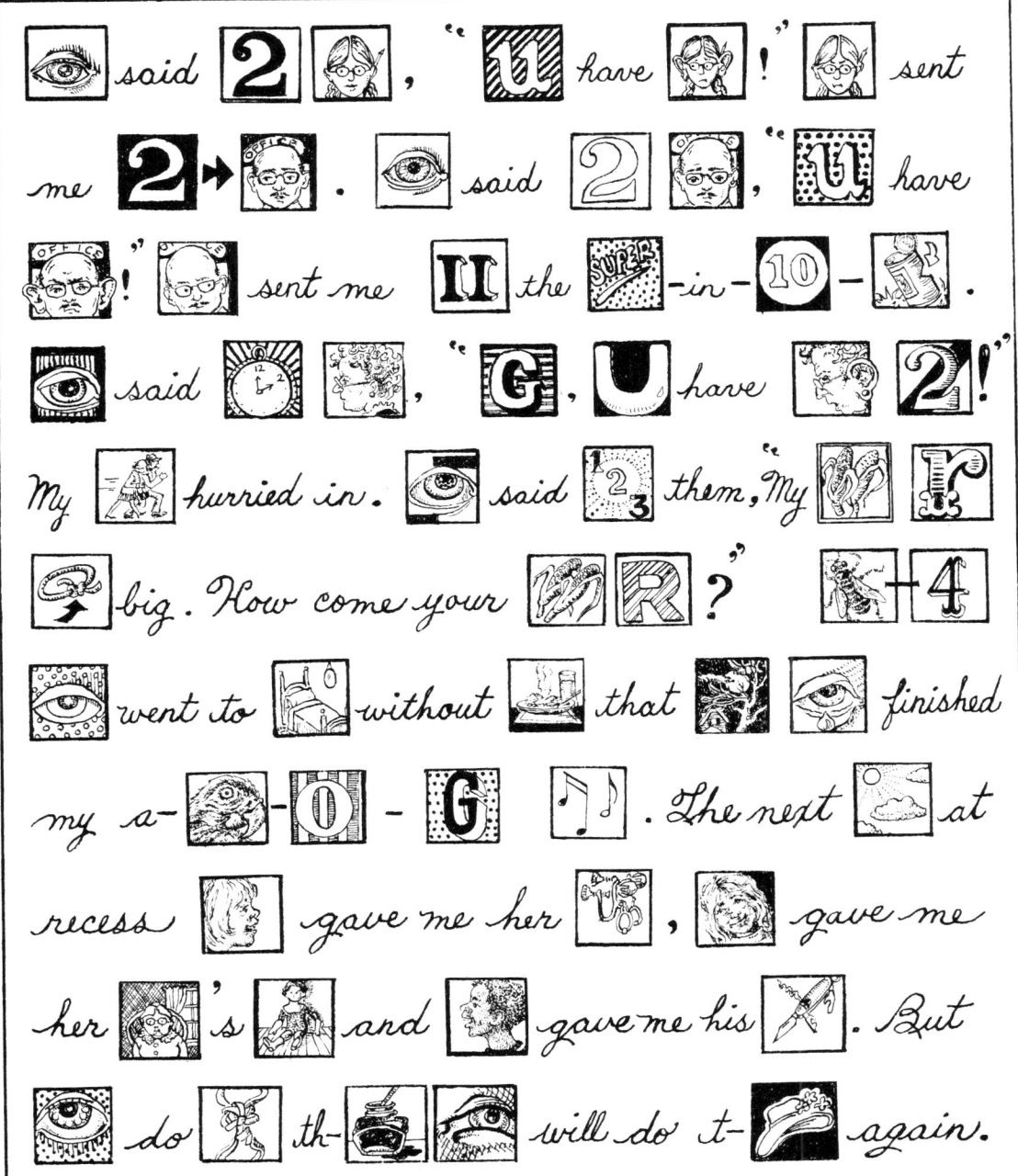

DOUBLE CROSTIC
10 A.M. Arlington Junior High School

Guess the words defined opposite and write them over their numbered dashes. Then transfer each letter to the correspondingly numbered square in the pattern. Black squares indicate word endings. The filled pattern will contain a quotation from Woodrow Wilson's second inaugural address. If this is a library book, or if this book belongs to your older brother, please use tracing paper.

A. Sit in your ___ ___ ___ ___, Tom Grout.
    99 7 63 51

B. They don't play banjos in Hawaii, they play ___ ___ ___ ___ ___ ___ ___ ___.
    115 126 60 13 24 27 121 161

C. Take the ___ ___ ___ down, Fowler. We're not playing volleyball today.
    3 66 110

D. 700 ___ ___ ___ ___ ___ ___ ___ ___ ___ by 4 equals 2,900. ___ ___ ___ ___ ___!
    41 55 105 22 145 87 72 18 112 15   143 11 39 102 57

E. Don't ___ ___ ___ ___ ___, Sarah.
    49 85 20 68 134

F. But I really don't ___ ___ ___ ___ well, Miss Simmons.
    69 94 14 61

G. I ___ ___ ___ ___ you she'd find out.
    150 130 71 37

H. His office is crazy. It's all dark and dusty. There are heaps of bones and skulls lying all around. It's like the ___ ___ ___ ___ ___ ___ ___ ___ ___.
    45 10 90 158 33 128 40 6 156

I. You're ikky, Jane Wilcox. I ___ ___ ___ ___ you.
    23 124 84 152

J. Name five countries which border the Mediterranean ___ ___ ___, Mary.
    8 86 30

K. Ha. Geez. Look what Sam ___ ___ ___.
    113 46 89

L. President Franklin D. Roosevelt ___ ___ ___ ___ on April 12, 1945.
    1 44 95 127

M. Samuel Cohn, what are you hiding under your ___ ___ ___ ___?
    151 56 140 96

N. a b c d e f g h ___ j k l m n ___ p q r s t u v w x y z.
    75   59

O. Samuel Cohn, ___ ___ ___ ___ ___ up!
    116 12 88 43 123

P. ___ ___ ___ ___ ___ is the opposite of light.
    17 160 97 108 53

Q. It's not a toad, Miss Simmons, it's a ___ ___ ___ ___.
    81 122 25 77

R. Tom Grout, will I have to ___ ___ ___ ___ ___ ___ ___ you to your desk like a horse?
    52 137 93 26 155 19 132

S. My brother told me that once when Miss Simmons was teaching first ___ ___ ___ ___ ___ a boy sassed her, and she lifted him right up out of his chair and turned him ___ ___ ___ ___ ___ -turvy.
    159 83 107 100 48   146 54 136 21 98

T. Yeah, but I'd still rather have her ___ ___ ___ Miss Carter.
    131 92 118 76

U. ___ ___ ___ me! Miss Carter doesn't pinch as hard.
    129 70 91

V. Yeah? Then why'd you ___ ___ ___ ___ "___ ___!" when she pinched your ear yesterday?
    31 109 133 36 101 74

W. ___ ___ ___ is that man or whom is ___ ___ ___ ___ man?
    29 58 82   120 62 144 16

X. I'll throw it so it ___ ___ ___ ___ ___ against the blackboard, but I won't throw it at her.
    154 80 64 111 135 157

Y. 100 times 100,000 equals ___ ___ ___ ___ ___ ___ ___.
    32 4 34 139 79 103 114 73

Z. All right. Who threw the peanut ___ ___ ___ ___ ___ ___ sandwich? I am ___ ___ ___ ___ ___ ___ disgusted with all of ___ ___ ___.
    65 148 5 47 106 153   42 9 104 67 125 138 28   78 2 35

*. Hey Bill, I'll ___ ___ ___ ___ you to the water fountain.
    149 142 38 117

♥. ___ ___ ___ ___ fo fum.
    147 141 119 50

101

THE CHINESE DEMON MAZE

DRAW A PICTURE

Take a piece of tracing paper, and cover this space. On the paper draw a picture of yourself.

DECODE THIS MESSAGE

Wvxlwrmtgsrhnvhhztvrhzdzhgvlugrnv.

QUIZ

On a separate piece of paper list the correct answers.

A. If my brother's name was Panyiotis, my name would be
   1. George.
   2. Harry.
   3. Lefty Myers.
B. Now that you have drawn a picture of yourself in the square on this page, *The Portmanteau Book* is
   1. funnier.
   2. sadder.
   3. uglier.
   4. upside down.
   5. sexier.
   6. banned in Las Vegas.
   7. worth more.
   8. worth less.
   9. worth about the same.
   10. Dullsville, U.S.A.
   11. a suitable present for the richest girl in the world to give her horse next Christmas.

C. If I went to the door, and it was an FBI agent and he said, "This is the FBI. Please call your father. I want to arrest him in connection with the notorious fried-egg conspiracy," I would
   1. call my mother.
   2. pretend I'm deaf.
   3. let go of our dog's collar.
   4. try to pin the rap on Mr. Foster, who lives next door.
   5. show the FBI agent the cellar door and say, "Dad's down there, sir," and then lock the door after him and flush the key down the toilet.
   6. keep insisting that we don't want anything today, thank you, no, not today, thank you; thank you, we don't want anything today, thank you, no. Could you come back next week?

D. If my mother said, "Taradiddle!" to me every day when I came into the kitchen after school, I would
   1. stop going to school so I wouldn't have to come home in the afternoon.
   2. walk in backwards so she would think I was leaving instead of coming in.
   3. call Macy's and ask them to send me a new mother right away.
   4. buy a bullhorn and when she said, "Taradiddle!" to me, say,

TARADIDDLE YOURSELF!

   5. tie a string around my finger to remind myself never to invite my friends home after school.

E. If I owned the world, I would
   1. send my parents away to boarding school.
   2. install a coin machine like the ones on public toilets on the door of every kid's room so that when his mother wants to come in, she has to pay 10¢. If the kid's inside, of course, it'll say OCCUPIED, and she'll have to come back later.
   3. worry about who to leave the world to in my will.
   4. in movie theaters make everyone over four feet tall unscrew their heads and hold them in their laps so they won't block the view of any kids sitting behind them.
   5. buy a castle. On the top floor there'll be a movie theater where I can go anytime I want and order up any movie I want, and an electric-train room, and a free soda fountain, and a rocket and model building room with a trap door to the launch pad on the roof. On the ground floor there'll be the kitchens and a library and closets and the bathroom and bedrooms for all my friends under fourteen, and a reception room for my parents to wait in when they come to visit, and a huge, colossal free toy store with five of everything and new stuff coming in every day and no salesmen sneaking around peering at you over boxes. In the cellar there'll be the armory and a chemistry and explosives lab and a gymnasium and swimming pool. In the rows of garages there'll be Harley-Davidson motorcycles and dune buggies and Ferraris and Corvettes and dragsters. On the south lawn there'll be a helicopter pad with my own helicopter and crew always ready. There'll be football and baseball and soccer fields, a tennis court, Ping-Pong, two lakes stuffed with fish. Every night there'll be a fireworks

display. Movie stars and generals and admirals will come for visits. In every room there'll be an icebox loaded with root beer and fried chicken and Mars Bars and apples and potato chips and ice cream and pickles. There'll be an airshow every weekend, marching bands and bagpipers on alternate Tuesdays. . . . And no matter what happens, nobody will turn us into donkeys like the boys in *Pinocchio*.

Essay Question: please answer the following questions in 2000 words or less. Essays should be submitted to W. Astebasket, Editorial Department, Little, Brown and Company, for judging.

If your dog is a terrier, not a Doberman pinscher (even though her name is Lassie), and you are walking up Mount Fujiama at three and one half miles per hour, will a Chevrolet truck rolling out of control down Pike's Peak reach the bottom by 4:30?

1. If not, why not?
2. If why, why not not?
3. Why not if, if not if?
4. If not why, why not?
5. Why not if not, if if not?
6. If not why, why not if?
7. If if, why not why?
8. Why if, not why if?

LOONY BIN

"Where is Kabul, Betty?"

"Afaganistan?"

"Miss Wilson. Miss Wilson. Miss Wilson. Miss Wilson. Miss Wilson. Miss Wilson. Miss Wilson. Miss Wilson. Miss Wilson. Miss Wilson. Miss Wilson. Miss Wilson. Miss Wilson."

"Children! Stop it! One at a time!"

"Geez, I only wanted to . . ."

"Why're you yelling at *me*, Miss Wilson? I was just . . ."

"That's not fair, Miss Wilson, it was . . ."

"Don't growl at me, Miss Wilson, it was Larry who . . ."

"CHILDREN!"

"Boy."

"Gee."

"Okay."

"Whooeee."

"Harold, *please.*"

"Me, Miss Wilson? I was just coughing. I got this cough."

"Harrold Carswell or Harold Clark, Miss Wilson?"

"Yeah, because Harrold Carswell lives in Florida. He's the fella that used to be a judge, Miss Wilson."

"And Clarkie's home sick today."

"Good old Clarkie."

"Yeah. I wonder what he's doing now."

"Probably reading a comic book and eating bananas."

"His mother's real funny, Miss Wilson, she thinks you can cure anything by eating bananas."

"She's real dumb, Miss Wilson."

"CHILDREN!!!"

"We're listening, Miss Wilson!"

"Yeah, come on, everybody, Miss Wilson's talking. Cut out the noise."

"Hey, Cathy, shut up, will ya? Miss Wilson's talking."

"Knock it off, Joe, it's Miss Wilson's turn."

"Go ahead, Miss Wilson, don't mind him. We're listening."

"Yeah, speak right up, Miss Wilson; he don't talk loud. His whole family's got laryngitis."

"And his father sucks eggs."

"Yeah, and his mother lays them."

Ha Ha.   Hee.   Ho.

"Hey, get off me, Joe, will ya?"

"*Why'd you say my mother laid eggs?*"

"Geez, I was *joking*. I was trying to make Miss Wilson laugh."

"Yeah, she don't look so good today, even for a substitute."

"Miss Wilson, Donnie's right, you don't look so good. Maybe you ought to go up to the Nurse's office. I'll take over if you want."

"Yeah, let Judy take over."

"That dumby?"

"CHILDREN CHILDREN CHILDREN CHILDREN *CHILDREN*!"

"*Okay.*"

"So why didn't you just *ask* us?"

"Geez."

"Lawrence Gutterman, how do you pronounce the name of the country of which Kabul is the capital?"

"You mispronounced my name, Miss Wilson. It's Guiterman, not Gutterman."

"The name of the country, Lawrence."

"Could you just try pronouncing my name right first, Miss Wilson? It's awful to have your name mispronounced. It really embarrasses me. Could you just try it?"

"Guiterman."

"Oh. Yeah. Say she got it right. Don, she got it right. First time."

"Second time. She fouled up when she called . . ."

"DONALD! Now. Lawrence. The name of the country of which Kabul is the capital."

"Afganustun."

"Miss Wilson.

Miss Wilson.

Miss Wilson.

Miss Wilson.

Miss Wilson.

Miss Wilson.

Miss Wilson.

Miss Wilson."

"Ha, ha. Geez, *he* mispronounced it, too."

"That's a awful dumb row, Miss Wilson."

"They need special work, Miss Wilson."

"HAROLD! THOMAS! WILLIAM! BACK TO YOUR SEATS!!"

"And let them get away with that, Miss Wilson?"

"You going to let them insult us like that, Miss Wilson?"

"Hey, come on, you guys, cut it out, she's beginning to cry."

"Yeah, come on, leave her alone."

"Have a heart."

"Yeah, and I'll bet she doesn't even know her slip's showing."

"Don't cry, Miss Wilson, she didn't mean it."

"It's not showing much."

"You want me to punch her for you, Miss Wilson?"

"Yeah? You and what other six guys?"

"C h i l d r e n ,
p l e a s e ,
o h   p l e a s e ,
b e   g o o d."

"Come on, Joe, cut it out!"

"Yeah, can't you see she's beginning to shake?"

"Geez, Joe, you'll have old Morris down on us like last time. He'll put us all on detention for a week."

"Yeah."

"No more."

"Everybody cut it out."

"Okay, Miss Wilson, we're ready."

"Okay, shoot, Miss Wilson."

. . . .

"She ain't recovered yet."

"Do you think she's sinking?"

"Come on, what was the last question? Maybe if we answer it, she'll stop sinking."

"Kabul. Where's Kabul?"

"Ain't he home sick today, like Clarkie?"

"Good old Clarkie."

"Yeah."

"Come on, come on. Answer the question. Bill, it's your turn."

"Afagunistan?"

"Afagunistan. Har-de-har-har. Him, too."

"He mispronounced it, too, Miss Wilson."

"Yeah, look at him; he's all blushing and everything."

"Boy, that is the *dumbest* row."

"Afagunistan. That's worse than you did, Dave."

"Me?" I ain't opened my mouth yet. It was Sheila."

"I guess I know how to pronounce
a simple word like that."
"How? How?"
"Yeah, how, smarts?"
"Afagunistum."
"Oh boy."
"Listen to *her*."
"Hey, Miss Wilson, you there? Did you hear Sheila?"
"I don't think she's listening."
"Is she still down behind her desk?"
"Maybe she crawled out the door
while we were talking."
"Have a look, Bill."
. . . . .
"Yeah, she's down there."
"What's she doing?"
"Geez, you know they're getting a worse class of substitute every year."
"Yeah, our parents oughta complain.
Paying good money for teachers
like that."
"What's she doing, Bill?"
"Shivering."
"She quit crying?"
"I can't see nothing but her back.
She's all huddled over."
BRAAAAAAAAAAAAAANGGG!
"School's out!"
"Let's go!"
"Hey, Larry: Turner's lot. We're playing this afternoon."
"Night, Miss Wilson."
"Night, Miss Wilson, that was a real good class today."
"Yeah, we really enjoyed it."
"Hey, let's go Mets!"

Breaking Loose

An Epic (though of modest proportions

I.

Albert Stangway
fell off the gangway,
bobbing up like a suckling
pig with a grapefruit
in his mouth.

He drifted south
with the oil slicks
and potato peelings,
waving feebly. Gulls
flapped and dove. The setting
sun winked
in the windows of skyscrapers.

Clinging to a plank,
he watched the running
sign at Palisades Amusement Park.
Gulls beaked
the grapefruit
out of his mouth.
He began to shout.
But by then he was off Hoboken
on the ebbing tide.

Riding
a packing case,
he swept past Ellis
Island. In the darkness,
while the waves lapped
and slapped
at the sides
of the packing case
        stenciled:

NOTTINGHAM ASHTRAYS

he drifted through the distant panoply
of lights: Wall Street,
stuttering
traffic signals, the glare
of a welder on a dock
like a luminous onion,
row on row on row
of floodlit two-family houses . . .
A traffic jam
on the Belt Parkway
leaked
cars south. He sobbed.

The lights glittered across the water
toward him.
The packing case bobbed
in the wakes of passing tugboats,
freighters, the *Queen of Bermuda*
outward bound like an incandescent fruitcake.

The faint ta-ra
of horns receded. The lights
winked out behind him. Alone
on the dark sea
he scrounged into a corner
of the packing case
and dozed through the night.

II.

An immensity
of sky
      and sea
spread round him.
             No gull
or bobbing orange. He raised
his shirt upon a pole. The dull
sea stank and glittered.

"I'm the last person on earth,"
he said aloud. "Lichen
thickens
over the island of rubble
which was New York City;
the ruins of Chicago
scum Lake Michigan;
stock pens
crumble
in Des Moines; the bombers bleed
rubber and insulation
onto the Tarmac
in Saskatchewan;
ice clogs
the oil derricks off Alaska;
the Trans-Siberian
Railway rusts
over ten thousand horizons;
Paris sleeps,
roofless, still;
from gutted London
wind sweeps
across the blackened ash
of Wales; Dublin,
like the shell
of a dead turtle,
gleams."

Crouched
in the packing case, he dreamed
of butter swimming
on milky oatmeal, of a haddock
steaming
crisp-eyed in frills of parsley, of horseradish sauce streaming
                  CHUG CHUG
down the eroded crags
and spires of a boiled beef

                    CHUG CHUG
of bag
puddings leaking CHUG CHUG
CHUG CHUG CHUG CHUG CHUG CHUG

The fishing boat wallowed
beside the packing case.

SANTA LUZIA
LISBOA

III.
After herring, bread
and coffee,
the captain slapped his back
and led
him out on deck again.

Rain
wrinkled the oily sea.
The crew cheered
as he was lowered by two sailors
into the packing case,
and cheered again
as the captain
handed him down
a slicker stenciled:

SANTA LUZIA
LISBOA

The lines were cleared.
The packing case drifted
into the rain.

He glanced
down at the demijohns
of water and stacks
of salted herring

at his feet
and then back at
the receding captain
beaming
and nodding at the rail.

He screamed.

The crew cheered.

The sea boiled
at the stern of the *Santa Luzia*.
The rainy air throbbed.
While he screamed and gestured,

the   **SANTA LUZIA**
               LISBOA

with its crew coiling the lines,
vanished into the fog.

IV.
He fell onto his knees
among the demijohns
and laid his forehead
on a crusty herring.

"They thought
I wanted to be
the first
to sail the North Atlantic
in a packing
case."

He misered
water. His hair
lanked down his neck and itched
with sea-lice and the salt.

In storms
the packing case pitched
and yawed
and spun. Ice
coated the herrings.
The salt spray
froze on his hair
and cheeks. He wept,
bailing with his hat.

His hands and feet were splotched
with white-rimmed sores. Dawn
gleamed
through a rift
in the blitzkreig
of cloud. His nose dripped
onto the herring
as he savaged it
with his teeth.

V.

In air
like melting
ice cream, the Azores
loomed
like camels' humps
out of the spring sea, azure,
sparkling.

He replenished his demijohns
during squalls, husbanding
his herring
by fishing over the side,
tasting
everything,
tacking the strangest heads
onto the sides of the packing case to dry.

Now and then,
as he lay draped against the demijohns,
gazing up into the black, starlit sky,
he wondered idly
if his mother had gotten over
missing him.

He cut his toenails
with the Portuguese fishknife,
his hair blowing around his face.

For hours, hanging
over the side, he watched the dim
phosphorescent turmoil
of the night sea, huge shadows sliding
by, sudden glowings and sparks.

VI.

A canary
lit
and pecked
at one of the fish heads.

The packing case
bumped
and then began to squeak
rhythmically.
Clambering out,
he waded through the lava rocks
to shore.

The pads
of his feet bruised
and sore, panting
painfully, he climbed through
the orchard of fig trees.
Far below, beached
above the roar
and geyser
of the surf,
the *Queen of Nottingham*
dried yellowly
in the sun.

In Arrecife, by drawing
pictures, he purchased
planks,
timbers, tools, leaving
the carter
at the outskirts of the city
to return to telegraph
his parents.

The police
found him two days later,
just finishing the
Queen of Nottingham's
outrigger.
    A celebrity,
though under surveillance till
his parents' arrival, he roamed
the streets, surreptitiously
purchasing supplies through the carter,
whom he had bribed
with the funds cabled
by his parents.

VII.

Down the stable
roof into the waiting arms
of the fig tree,
he slid.

Rockets cabled up
through the night.
The park clapped
and danced. A haze
of torchlight
hung above the trees.

He ran quietly
through the deserted
streets, slid
into the warm garbagy
water of the harbor.

The *Queen of Nottingham*
glided darkly under
the stern of the Spanish destroyer
moored at the breakwater.

VIII.

Two months later,
off French Guiana,
his parents conferred
with him aboard the British aircraft carrier,
Hornet.

His father angrily
insisted
he have a haircut.
His mother sniveled.

Assisted
by a chief petty officer
and two ratings,
he made necessary
adjustments
to the *Queen of Nottingham*'s rudder,
and ten days later
was observed off Jamaica,
tacking
to windward.

BONUS! BONUS! BONUS! BONUS! BONUS! BONUS! BONUS! BONUS! BONU

SEVEN BONUS PAGES!

(N.B.: These seven bonus pages contain page 11,004 and an exciting chase)

CRAZY TOM *(continued from page 30)*

Roaring like a wounded musk ox, Crazy Tom heaved up out of his sleep, grappling at the air, his bloodshot eyes bulging.

I grabbed Harvey's arm, yanking him out of reach; we fled down the stairs. Behind us the stairway thundered and creaked. I glanced back Crazy Tom was lumbering after us. Suddenly he stumbled, fell, started to roll . . .

"Back against the wall!" I yelled. "We'll be crushed!"

Tumbling head over heels, his feet in the air, Crazy Tom grabbed a beam; the beam cracked; a cascade of plaster and laths poured down over him.

Coughing, choking, we peered through the clouds of dust; chunks of plaster rained down on our heads. A monstrous, jagged hole gaped in the wall of the staircase.

"He's fallen right through!" said Arlo.

"Look!" yelled John.

In the door at the bottom of the stairs Crazy Tom loomed like a ghost, white with plaster dust from head to foot.

"Back onto the roof!" I yelled.

But the stairs were blocked with rubble.

Crazy Tom spoke,

"Come. Come. Why you 'fraid? Tom good."

He beckoned to us.

We huddled together on the stairs.

"We got no choice," I whispered. "We're trapped."

Arlo nodded.

"We better humor him."

(N.B.: Very few books have a page 11,004. Dictionaries, multivolume encyclopedias, telephone directories—even these giants of the publishing world often find themselves ignominiously ending at page (sneer) eight-thousand-and-two or (shame! shame!) four-thousand-three-hundred-and-one.)

John and Arlo and me started slowly down the stairs toward Crazy Tom. Harvey stayed behind, crouching, quietly trying to cover himself with broken laths and bits of paneling. As we neared the bottom, Crazy Tom backed away. We came out of the stairway and stopped, watching him. On his left arm blood ran, bright red against the white plaster dust.

"Hi," I croaked.

"Candy. Candy." He gestured toward the room beside the stairway. We backed into it. I glanced behind me. No doors. We were trapped. Our only chance was if Harvey snuck out behind him and ran for help. Crazy Tom waddled after us.

"Candy. Candy. I bring."

He plunged both hands into the bib front of his overalls, coming up with two dripping fistfuls of candy bars, reaching out, raining them down in front of us.

"Take some," I whispered. "We've got to humor him."

Arlo handed me an Almond Joy, John a Milky Way. We tore the paper off with our teeth, watching Crazy Tom.

"Give *him* some," whispered Arlo.

I reached down and picked up a big fifty-cent Hershey bar.

"Here," I said. "For you. You eat, too. Catch."

He grinned. I tossed it to him. He caught it and still grinning, took a huge bite, wrapper and all.

I glanced around. Even the window was boarded up.

"Maybe it'll be all right," whispered Arlo. "Yeah," I whispered, smiling and nodding, "till one of us blinks the wrong way."

Then, *Bloom!* he'd go berserk and tear us all limb from limb.

I kept glancing around, trying to figure a way out. Hey! . . . maybe . . . it was our only chance anyway: a heating duct . . . about two feet around . . . of course, we didn't know where it'd lead to . . . still . . .

"Sit. You sit. Eat. More. More."

He dumped more fistfuls of candy bars on the rubbishy floor. We crouched down. He watched us, grinning. My throat was so dry I could hardly swallow. I could have been eating sawdust for all I knew.

"Behind us," I whispered to Arlo and John out of the corner of my mouth. "The big pipe. If he starts for us."

"You sit, too," said Arlo to Crazy Tom.

Crazy Tom started to lower himself down, one hand gripping the door jamb . . .

"ORRRRRRRGGGGHHHHH!"

Maybe his hand had struck a splinter on the door jamb, maybe he'd sat down on a piece of broken glass: we didn't wait to find out.

"He's *cracked*!" yelled Arlo, clambering over me, his feet in my stomach.

All three of us scrambled toward the heating duct, clawing, yelling, and dived in . . . .

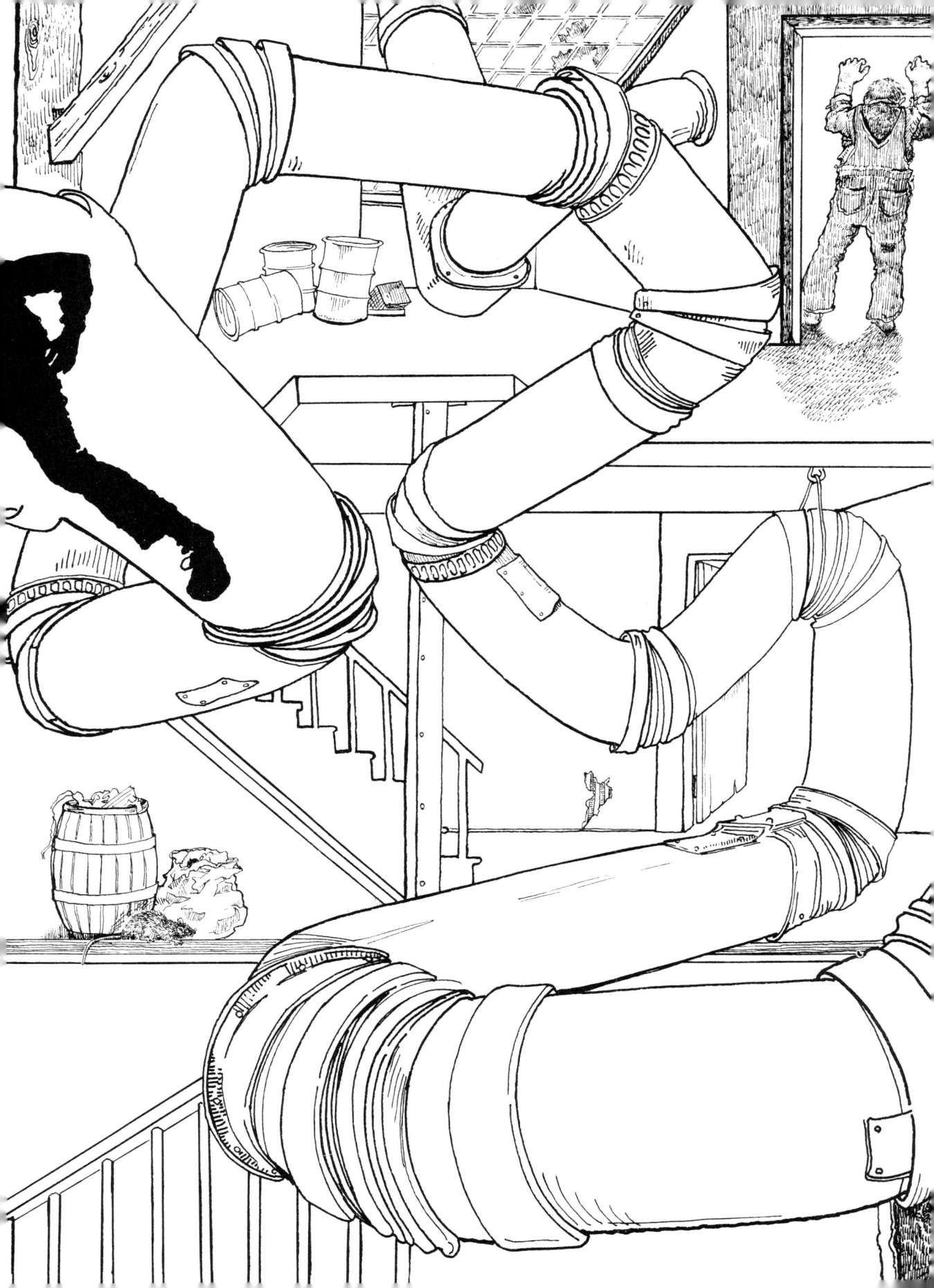

THE END

HOT IV: LOVE

We straggled along Cort Street. It was as hot as the inside of a Mexican pepper. It was as hot as a toad's belly. It was as hot as a rotting radish. It was *almost* as hot as six teachers losing their tempers all at once at you on a hot day.

As we limped around the side of Joe's house toward the garage, a voice cried from a cellar window:

"Oh Momma, he's purchased the mortgage on our house and unless I marry him, he's going to evict us, even though it's snowing out, look Momma, and thundering and lightning and the wind's tearing up the sidewalk in chunks."

"Well, I'm sure," replied another voice.

"Who's that?" I said.

"I don't know," said Joe.

We all stopped.

"Now Maybelle, you got to decide," said a gruff voice. "It's me or the slushy streets."

"No, no."

"Aw," said Joe. "It's my sisters. They're rehearsing a play."

"Let's listen."

We crouched down around the cellar window.

"Kiss me."
"MAAAAAAAAAAAAMA!"
Sputter. Cough.

"Peggy, does there have to be all this kissing? I mean, it's just Jane Turner in my brother's old trousers with a yukky beard made out of your grandmother's fur coat, and it's no fun at all. Couldn't we just, you know, shake hands?"

Scream. Bang. Kick.

"There! You can write it yourselves! I tried and tried and tried, I got up before it was light all week so I could finish in time! And this is the thanks I get! Yah, yah. Can't we just shake hands? Whoever heard of lovers shaking *hands*, Alice Insull? Whoever heard of that?"

"Oh smarty Peggy Milspaugh. Thinks she knows everything. Elizabeth-Taylor-shook-hands-with-Richard-Burton-millions-of-times-in-that-movie-on-TV-last-week. And they were *unmarried* lovers."

"Yes, but they did kiss a lot, too, Alice," said her sister Jane. "Be fair."

"Kiss-shmish. Peggy said lovers don't shake hands, but *they* did."

"She meant lovers don't shake hands during crises. Come on. It doesn't *hurt* you to kiss Tom Throat once in a while. You have the best part anyway."

So Peggy yelled: "I won't go on till Alice apologizes and promises not to criticize so much!"

So then there was a lot of whispering, the others persuading Alice to apologize, I guess, because pretty soon she said,

"Okay. I won't criticize anymore. As long as I don't have to kiss Jane in rehearsals, only during the performances."

So Peggy said all right and they started again.

"Marry me, sweet Maybelle," said the gruff voice.

"But I love Tom Throat, Mr. Germ."

"Throat? Germ?" whispered Albert.

"Peggy likes names that express character," said Joe, grinning.

"Tom Throat!" cried the gruff voice. "The name makes me gargle! What's he got that I haven't?"

"Youth! And love! And beauty!" trilled Alice Insull.

"Pfaugh! What's beauty when the coal scuttle's empty and the hearth's slippery with hoarfrost? You'd be better off sprawling on Turkish cushions before a roaring fire, cracking roasted chestnuts with an old toad like me."

"Oh dear. And love?"

"What's love when you glance up from slicing a frozen parsnip into the kitchen sink and spy the rats fleeing the sinking

126

house across the icy fields. You'd be better off setting a steaming bubbling roast beef before a bald old possum like me."

"Oh dear. And youth?"

"What's youth when icicles hang from your husband's young nose as he spoons stale Wheaties between his chapped lips and there comes a knock at the door and it's the neighborhood children to ask if they can skate in your living room again? You'd be better off basking on the beach in Miami while a hairy-nosed old trout like me rubs suntan lotion on your knuckles."

"Oh dear."

"I ain't so bad. Take . . ."

CRASH! SPLINTER! BANG!

"Unhand my love, my ladybug, my mouse, my flower!"

"Tom Throat!"

"Tum Troat!"

Pow! Sock! Tinkle! Splinter! CRASH!

Smacked lips.

"I fixed him, Maybelle, there's nothing more to fear. I, Tom Throat, have redeemed the mortgage and your honor."

"But how, Tom?"

"Oil, Maybelle, oil! My ranch is floating on a pool of oil. I've been setting up all morning with Mr. Vanderbilt and the King of England, drawing the contract. I've sold out for seventeen zillion dollars for me and heaps of diamonds and French gewgaws for you. There ain't *nothing* I can't buy, Maybelle. Look at those Cadillacs and Rolls-Royces and Boeing 747s, those snowmobiles and dune buggies and mobile homes parked outside. They're *mine*! I bought 'um all this morning. Now I'm all wore out. I got to rest. This afternoon I aim to buy a *country*. Something medium-sized and warm in winter. Guatemala, maybe, except I doubt the United Fruit Company would sell. Oh Maybelle, Maybelle, *Maybelle*!"

Click. Zzzzzzzz.

The strains of the wedding march floated up through the cellar window.

"And so," crooned Peggy, "Tom Throat and Maybelle Neck were married, and so were Maybelle's mother, Agnes Peacorn, and Silas Germ, who reformed and dandled Maybelle's children on his old white knee."

Applause. Whistling.

Then Joe yelled into the cellar.

"Tom Throat chews tobacco!"

"And doesn't wash his feet!" I shouted.

"He's got a hairy belly!" yelled Albert.

"Bloo bloo!" yelled Tim.

Confused screams, crashes.

"Let's go!" I yelled.

We rounded the house. Joe's father was just locking the garage. Albert and Tim and me kept going over the board fence, yelling goodbye to Joe and hello to his father, plunging through Mrs. Lingleman's wet sheets, up Laughton Road, Albert sheering off on Beach Drive, Tim and me slowing panting to a walk.

"Isn't it all supposed to have a moral?" asked Tim. "I mean, shouldn't everything add up to something?"

"Not when it's this hot," I said.

We trudged up the driveway to supper.

Consolation Page

(*continued from page 141*)   And so the crocodile, with oozing jaws, was led away by elements of the 101st Airborne, 5th Air Cavalry, and 301st Field Artillery, as the last chorus of "Row, Row, Row Your Boat" echoed through the smoky vaults behind them.

EDITOR'S NOTE: *Due to a printer's error, page 141 has been omitted from this edition of* The Portmanteau Book. *Thus, all but the opening paragraphs and the last sentence of* The Crocodile *are lacking. This unfortunate omission may, however, be turned to your advantage. If, for instance, you are someday caught in English class with an essay or story to write and nothing to write about, your brain as empty as the cardboard boxes heaped outside the back door of a supermarket, complete* The Crocodile. *Describe what happened on that fateful day between the time the door of the classroom banged open and in rushed . . . who? and the final dénouement . . . Why is everybody singing "Row, Row, Row Your Boat?" Where did all the smoke come from? Vaults? The 101st Airborne?*

If you receive a good mark on the essay or story — say, ninety or above — please be generous. Send five or ten points — you'll still have a B or B+ — to the publisher, and we will distribute them to needy children all over the world.

Answers to Big Bonus Game Section

- *The Rebus:* I said to Miss Carstairs, "You have big ears." She sent me to the principal. I said to him, "You have big ears." He sent me to the Superintendent. I said to her, "Gee, *you* have big ears, too!" My parents hurried in. I said to them, "My ears are not big. How come your ears are?" Before I went to bed without supper that night I finished my apology notes. The next day at recess Janie gave me her bracelet, Helen gave me her pearl earrings, Anne gave me her grandmother's doll, and George Katz gave me his Swiss army knife. But I don't think I will do it again.

- *The Double-Crostic:* A. seat; B. ukuleles; C. net; D. multiplied *and* wrong; E. whine; F. feel; G. told; H. catacombs; I. hate; J. Sea; K. has; L. died; M. hand; N. i *and* o; O. stand; P. heavy; Q. frog; R. harness; S. grade *and* topsy; T. than; U. Not; V. yellow; W. who *and* that; X. mushes; Y. 10,000,000; Z. butter, utterly, *and* you; *. race; ♥ fe *and* fi.

- *The Code:*
  a=z   b=y   c=x   d=w   etc.

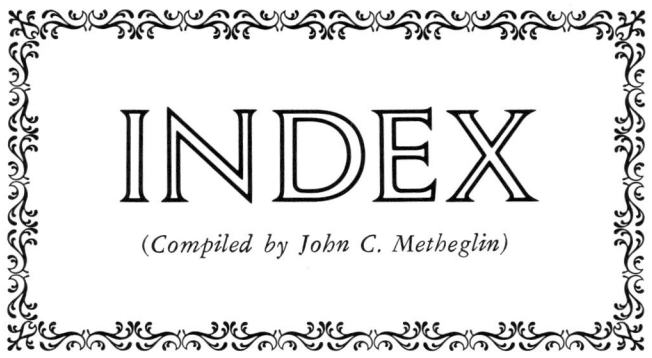

Browsers Welcome

(Persons wishing to benefit from this index are advised to start with the first entry, Abbott, F. C., and follow it faithfully from reference to reference. Other interesting entries are: Sex, Monday, Jokes, Metheglin, and Xerxes.)

A

Abbott, F. C. — Bank teller. Machine-gunned by Ralph (Mouthy) Max in left arm. *See* Robbery.

Advertisements — 36

Asylum, Ossining — Present home of Nelly R. Varner.

B

Bagels — *See* Lox.

Balsam, Ginger — *See* Sex.

Banfield, Laura M. — Collapsed during bank robbery and was dragged to safety in the vault by Harry Waters, whom she married two weeks later, grateful and adoring, in the Church of the Holy Synagogue, March 29, 1966. *See* Vault.

Boiled Kvetch — 87

Bonus Pages — 31–36, 48–49, 99–106, 11,004–123

Breaking Loose — 112

Brother's Hash — 92

C

Campbell's Soup, Beef Vegetable, can of. Empty crushed, iced by freezing rain late in the afternoon of March 24, 1966, it took J. C. Goldmeyer's feet out from under him. *See* Goldmeyer, J. C.

Candied Peach — 90

Comic Book — 31

Conroy, Betty M. — Housewife. Screamed and ran to hide during bank robbery, March 15, 1966. *See* Vault.

D

Deadwood — *See* pages 9–14, 35–41, 88, 99–103, etc.

Deinger, Buck — Bank robber. Hairy nose, crooked tobacco-stained teeth, snap-brim fedora, trench coat pockets stuffed with hand grenades. First apprehended Troy, New York, January 8, 1941, on a charge of stealing with intent to eat — two apricots and a pear from A. C. Napolitano's fruit stand. Many subsequent arrests. Yelled and gesticulated excitedly during robbery of First National Bank of Scarsdale. Present whereabouts unknown. *See* Max, Ralph (Mouthy). *But also see* Willard, Wm. E.

Diverted Haddock — 86

Dog, unidentified — Who nipped up the $10,000 deposit slip, fluttered by a sudden gust of wind from the pocketbook of Mrs. R. L. Underhill, and galloped away down Main Street, Scarsdale, with it, pursued by Mrs. Underhill heavily, silently, distraughtly, panting, weeping, staggering past Hackenfelt's Ford Agency, past Lungwell's Uniform Center, falling in front of Joe's Bar and Grill, watching helplessly as dog vanished across vacant lot behind laundromat. Late that night Mrs. Underhill was seen boarding a flight for Sao Paulo, Brazil, with a bulging suitcase, glancing back over her shoulder. *See* Scarsdale, town dump of.

E

End, The — 142
Entomological Soup — 85
Erickson, Sinn Fein — Said, "Gimme a light, will ya, Al?" to A. R. Tannahill, March 24, 1966, and having lit his cigarette, tossed away the burning $10,000 deposit slip, climbed back into his pick-up truck, and drove away through the smoke of the gently burning dump. However, *see* Rain.
Eyes — This page is now looking up into *your* eyes.

F

Foreword — 7
Friday — *See* Saturday.
Fried Hall Closet — 90
Fruit Kiss — 89

G

Germ, Silas — 126
Goldmeyer, J. C. — Jarred by his fall, he decided to quit work for the day and hobbling back to his truck, which was still half full of refuse from Penson's Department Store in New Rochelle, drove directly home and was put to bed with a hot beer by his wife Nancy Goldmeyer, *whom see.*
Goldmeyer, Nancy — Wife of J. C. Goldmeyer. While hanging up her husband's overalls in the closet, she discovered the remains of the $10,000 deposit slip stuck to the seat of the overalls. Two days later Wm. E. Willard, Sheriff of Westchester County, withdrew $1,000 from his new account at the First National Bank of Binghamton and the following Tuesday deposited it in the recently opened account of N. Goldmeyer at the First National Bank of Scarsdale, where the deposit was processed by teller Andrew Upshaw, *whom see.*
Grotowski, Paul — *See* Yarborough, Edith.

H

Hardware store — Sorry, closed today.
How the Pronouns Fell Out while the Nouns Were Away. . . . — 57
Humdrum — see pages 28–45, 54, 88–90, 102–105, etc.

I

Ice — 20
Imbs, J. C. — Judge of the Superior Court, Westchester County. October 21st, 1971: commended Andrew Upshaw, Oliver Jameson, Albert Ostreicher, and F. P. Loring. Recommended that L. Krepet be fired from his post as chief cashier, First National Bank of Scarsdale, for negligence. Sentenced Mrs. Nancy Goldmeyer, Wm. E. Willard, and, in absentia, Mrs. R. L. Underhill, Buck Deinger, Agnes Malbranch, and Ralph (Mouthy) Max to prison for complicity in the robbery of the First National Bank of Scarsdale (*which see*), March 15, 1966.
Indignation — 64
Infested Spinach — 91

J

Jaaaaaack Meeeears! — 112
Jokes — The compiler of this index, John C. Metheglin, wishes to report that after a diligent search, he can find no jokes. There are, he adds, many attempts, but these will only depress the reader by their sickly, limping, downcast demeanor and have not, therefore, been indexed.

K

Kabul — 107

Kander's, Colonel, Kentucky Fried, Chicken, wing. — Waved by Oliver Jameson, cousin of Albert Ostreicher, at a man in a black beard, low fedora, and dark glasses who had just entered the front section of the Colonel Kander's establishment. "What's old Willard doing up in these parts, Al?" "Old Willard who?" "Will Willard, the sheriff of Westchester County." Ostreicher turned to look. "That ain't old Willard." "Yes it is," said Jameson. "I'd recognize his cowboy boots anywhere. Sold them to him myself just before I quit working at Alton's." Ostreicher turned to look again. "Well, sure enough. You're right. What we better do?" *See* Varner, Nelly R.

Krepet, L. — Chief Cashier, First National Bank of Scarsdale. Pooh-poohed Andrew Upshaw's suggestion of foul play and immorality and advised him to tend to business. *See* Years, four.

L

Lanier, Gertrude — *See* Grotowski, Paul.

Liver Punishment — 88

Longest Word in the English language — 80

Loring, F. P. — Deputy Sheriff, Broome County. Extricated Wm. E. Willard from the screaming clutches of Nelly R. Varner in order to arrest him for impersonating an unknown man in a black beard, low fedora and dark glasses. Led the subsequent investigation into his true identity. *See* Imbs, J. C.

Los Angeles — *See* Smog.

Love — 124

Lox — *See* Bagels.

M

Malbranch, Agnes — Common-law wife of Buck Deinger.

Max, Ralph (Mouthy) — Bank robber. Livid raised scar on left cheek, ugly look in squinty eyes, chews cigar butt incessantly, often worked out with 30-caliber machine-gun at town dump, Scarsdale. Claimed to be practicing for the 1976 Olympics. F. C. Abbott, bank teller, rocking in his chair on his front porch, his left arm in a sling, disputes this claim, exhibiting a 30-caliber slug removed from his arm as evidence. Ralph (Mouthy) Max last seen speeding away up Cherry Street in a stolen blue 1963 Ford sedan driven wildly by Buck Deinger. Present whereabouts unknown. *But see* Willard, Wm. E.

Menu — 54

Metheglin, John C. — Compiler of this index and the foremost indexer on the East Coast. Rates: $1 per page. No poetry. References furnished.

Metheglin, Mary R. — Wife of the compiler. A careful housewife, loving mother, and fond wife.

Metheglin, Stanley Q. — Son of the compiler. Presently studying computer indexing at Valpariso (Illinois) Polytechnic Institute.

Metheglin, Virginia R. — Daughter of the compiler. Voted the prettiest girl in her class at Randolph-Macon High, 1965, now married to Walter Blumberg, CPA, and the mother of two fine boys.

Metheglin, Mrs. Wilbur, Sr. — Aging mother of the compiler. Can be seen most mornings taking her constitutional up and down on the sidewalk in front of her son's house in East Orange, New Jersey.

Monday — *See* Tuesday.

Mystery Page — 47

N

Nakedness — 10

Nakedness — complete: — 12–13
             partial: — 61–77
             mental: — 58

Norway — 61

Nose, funny — *See* mirror.

O

$1 + 1 = 0$ — 75

Onions — 50

Ostreicher, Albert — Who moved from Scarsdale to Binghamton on June 14, 1970, having decided to quit his uncle's hardware store and go into business for himself as a franchiser for Colonel Kander's Kentucky Fried Chicken. *See* Kander's, Colonel, Kentucky Fried, Chicken, wing.

P

Page 11,004 — *See* page 11,004
Parents' Goose — 89
Peacorn, Agnes — 128
Philosophy — Oh well, the book only cost about $4. What'd you expect for that, Mark Twain?
Portmanteau Book, The — *See* pages 124–127. (The author has informed the indexer that he wishes to disown pages 1–123 and 128–142.)

Q

Queen of Bermuda — 113
Queen of Nottingham — 116
Quist, Lawrence M. — Bank teller. Hid trembling and praying under counter during bank robbery. *See* Quist, Martin L.
Quist, Martin L. — Admiring son of L. M. Quist. Still firmly believes his father would have attacked and captured bank robbers if he had not tripped over a sack of money and, striking his forehead against an adding machine, rendered himself unconscious. *See*, however, Quist, L. M.

R

Rain — Which fell briefly March 24, 1966, snuffing out the flaming $10,000 deposit slip. Later turned to freezing rain. *See* Campbell's Soup, beef vegetable, can of.
Rasbore — Any of a genus of tiny, brilliantly colored cyprinid freshwater fishes often kept in the tropical aquarium.
Review Questions — 106
Robbery — *See* Scarsdale, First National Bank of.
Rundle, Harold B. — First Vice President. Hid his face in his hands and weeping, ran into the vault during bank robbery. *See* Vault.

S

Saturday — *See* Sunday.
Scarsdale, First National Bank of — held up March 15, 1966. *See* Deinger, Buck; Max, Ralph (Mouthy). *See also* Rundle, Harold B.; Conroy, Betty M.; Banfield, Laura F.; Quist, Lawrence M.
Scarsdale, Town Dump of — Where dog dropped the $10,000 deposit slip in favor of a lamb chop bone. Slip fluttered to rest by shoe of A. R. Tannahill, *whom see.*
SDRAWKCAB — 93
Sex — *See* Lanier, Gertrude.
Smog — *See* Los Angeles.
Soiled Eggs — 90
Squawwwk — *See* your local bookstore.
Sunday — *See* Monday

T

Tannahill, A. R. — Ignited $10,000 deposit slip on burning cottage cheese container, lit his cigar with it, and handing it to Sinn Fein Erikson (*whom see*), went back to stripping the lead from a rusty boiler.
Taste, poor — *See* pages 14–38, 52–61, 91–108, 153, 178–194, etc.
Thursday — *See* Friday.
Toiletpaper — 38
Tuesday — *See* Wednesday.

U

Underhill, Mrs. R. L. — Opened a savings account in the name of Wm. E. Willard, March 22, 1966, First National Bank of Binghamton, with an initial deposit of $10,000. Frequent companion of Wm. E. Willard at political clambakes and Knights of Columbus testimonial dinners. Now resides in Sao Paulo, Brazil. *See* Dog.
Underwear — *See* any good haberdashery.
Upshaw, Andrew — Novice teller at First National Bank of Scarsdale. Wondered why Sheriff Wm. E. Willard would pay an old, slop-shoed harridan like Mrs. Nancy Goldmeyer $1,000. Brought

the matter to the attention of his pince-nezed superior, L. Krepet, Chief Cashier, *whom see.*

Usher, Thomas — *See* Balsam, Ginger.

V

Vamp, The — 37

Varner, Nelly R. — Weirdo. On overhearing O. Jameson's and A. Ostreicher's conversation, she stopped gnawing on a drumstick and taking two pairs of handcuffs from her pocket, handcuffed herself first to the cash register and then to Wm. E. Willard. Screaming in a loud, raucous voice that President Roosevelt should be impeached, she began to do the Charleston. *See* Loring, F. P. *See also* Asylum, Ossining.

Vault — First National Bank of Scarsdale. Domicile of Betty M. Conroy, Harold B. Rundle, Laura F. Banfield, and Harry Waters from 2:15 P.M., March 15, 1966, when they ran inside during the bank robbery, and 8:41 A.M., March 16, when the time lock reopened, and they emerged hungry, thirsty, tearful, and distraught into the morning sunlight and the arms of their waiting families. *See* Robbery.

W

Watteau, Jean Antoine — (1684–1721) French painter.

Wednesday — *See* Thursday.

Willard, Wm. E. — Sheriff of Westchester County. Arrived at First National Bank of Scarsdale a few minutes too late to apprehend Buck Deinger and Ralph (Mouthy) Max, who had just fled with $50,000 in small, unmarked bills. *But see* Zutkowski, Willie M.

Wrenches — *See* Hardware store.

X

Xerxes Xenophon Gort — *See Rackety-Bang and Other Verses* at your local bookstore.

Y

Yarborough, Edith — *See* Usher, Thomas.

Years, four — which passed. *See now,* Ostreicher, Albert.

Z

Zutkowski, Willie M. — Received gaily wrapped gift package from Agnes' Malbranch, March 20, 1966, on the downtown platform of the 51st Street station of the Lexington Avenue subway in New York City. *See* Malbranch, Agnes. Later the same day Zutkowski turned the package over to his aunt, Mrs. R. L. Underhill (*whom see*) and was given a kiss and 50¢ for running her errand.

Zymurgy — The last word.

RESULTS OF A POLL

Editor's Note: At the fall 1973 conference of the American Traumatical Association in Atlanta, a speech by Thomas Rockwell, author of THE PORTMANTEAU BOOK, was interrupted by catcalls and derisive gestures. Mr. Rockwell, who had been peacefully speaking on "The Children of America and THE PORTMANTEAU BOOK. Will It Help?", asked for an explanation. After some commotion, during which the ushers ejected an unruly dog, a bearded gentleman stood on a chair and declared that he did not think that children would read the book — it was the wrong color, too heavy, and did not turn on and off like a television set.

"Come, come," cried Mr. Rockwell, and to back up his contention, offered to undertake a scientific poll of school children.

Some months later, in response to a letter inquiring about the progress of the poll, the following note was received:

> *Editer*
> *Little Brown and Co*
>
> *Dear Sir;*
> *Mr. Rockwell ain't here. He left last week unexpectedly for Sout America. He didn't leave no address or nothing, just a note asking me to come in. The only thing on his desk was these crunkled tape recurdings and pitchers. They was all crunkled when I found them. I didn't do it.*
>
> *Sinserely yrs,*
>
> *Samoth L. Lewkroc*

The transcript which follows was taken from these tapes. Some of the gaps in the transcript are the result of the poor condition of the tapes. Other gaps, marked by four dots, indicate garbled or inaudible sections.

ROCKWELL: *I mailed* THE PORTMANTEAU BOOK *to a randomly selected group of ten- to twelve-year-olds on April 12th. Today — April 26th — I'll station myself outside the school to question them.*

Here I am. It's a clear day, rather chilly. I'm glad I wore my long underwear. Oh. Here comes the first one, a boy — stocky, flop-haired, hands in pockets. Excuse me, could you tell me what you thought of THE PORTMANTEAU BOOK?

BOY 1: Well, my mother said I didn't have to read it if I'd eat my vegetables without bugging her for two weeks, she'd give me an excuse? So, geez, I was eating peas and beans and carrots and corn. Then she served fried eggplant.

"Eggplant isn't a vegetable," I said. "Look at it. It's fried. People don't fry vegetables. Did you ever hear of fried beans or fried peas?"

"Eat," she said.

So I threw down my napkin. "Geez, I'll read the book then. You said I either had to read the book or eat my vegetables, so I'll read the book."

Yeah, well, I read it all right — while I was eating the eggplant. But I don't remember much about it — the book, I meant, not the eggplant. I can still taste the eggplant — greasy, like thick, gooey, axle . . .

ROCKWELL: *Well, here's our second respondent, a girl — pretty, her arms full of schoolbooks. Excuse me . . .*

GIRL 1: THE PORTMANTEAU BOOK? I liked it a lot. I really did. I read it twice. I think it's a wonderful book. I liked everything about it. Do you remember the part where the first man, the one who'd been shipwrecked? where he rescued Friday from the cannibals? I think that was . . . . What? . . . . Oh. You mean that's not THE PORTMANTEAU BOOK? Really? Hm.

You mean that's not it *either*? You mean you're talking about *another* book?

Gosh, I . . . I guess I missed it then. I mean, I read all the time, but I can't . . . *Say!* It isn't the one where this girl falls down a rabbit hole? And then she . . .

ROCKWELL: *Here comes our third respondent, a boy — slouching along. Excuse me . . .*

BOY 2: Orglofug gamsol *cara-* smuglo -mel candy* slog *stuck* moglar *teeth can't* glogful *TALK!*

ROCKWELL: *This doesn't seem to be . . .*

Ohhhhhhhhhhhhhhhhhhhh, *sure*! I remember *now*! Oh boy, I really *loved* that book. I read it and read it. My mother kept asking me what I was laughing about. And wasn't that scary when Tom and Becky Thatcher got lost in the cave? My mother said I . . . .

Hey, I'll bet you're an *imposter.* I'll bet you're just *pretending* to work for the ASPCA. I'll bet you're one of those awful people my mother's always warning me about! DON'T YOU TOUCH ME! Mr. Wilson! Mr. Wilson! Mr. Wilson, there's a man out here pretending to . . .

(*tape mutilated*)

BOY 3: Do I get a prize if I liked it? . . . . Well, do I get a prize if I *didn't* like it? . . . . Aw, who cares? I didn't read it anyway.

(*tape mutilated*)

ROCKWELL: Um. Well, here . . . .

BOY 4: Whatta you mean? I didn't get any book in the mail. Are you a policeman? Who told you I got a book in the mail? Do I look like the kind of kid that reads books like that? If I got a book like that in the mail, I'd report it. I wouldn't even wait to put on my shoes. Soon as I saw what it was I'd run barefoot all the way to the police station. . . . What? THE PORTMANTEAU BOOK? You mean you're not a policeman? A pollster? What's that? . . . . And you can't ever tell what I say to you? Not even to Mr. Wilson or my father? And you can't arrest me? No kidding.

Geez, wait'll I tell you then. Ha. See, I don't know anything about *your* book, I might of got it, I might not, but about three weeks ago Tom Sykes and me was out behind his garage going through the trash because the

GIRL 2: Excuse me, are you from the ASPCA? Because I'm the girl who called about the . . . .
Book? What book? I didn't say anything about a book. I called about a dog. There's this dog shut up in a car behind the school? On Elm Street? And he's been there all day, ever since . . . . What do you keep talking about a book for? It was a *dog.* I don't see what any *book* has to do with it. Why do you work for the ASPCA if all you can think about is books? You should work in a library or something. How can you think about books anyway, when that dog is . . .

night before his father'd thrown out all his comic books. And we found this advertisement, one of those that comes in two envelopes? one inside the other? and on the inside one it says, DO NOT OPEN UNLESS YOU ARE OVER TWENTY-ONE YEARS OF AGE? Anyway, inside there was this ad for *The Kama Sutra, The Indian Book of Love.* It said they'd send it to you for five days free. So geez, we figured what the heck, we can read it and then send it back and it won't cost us anything. So we did, and *wow!* you should see it; it's pretty good. I mean you can't understand it too well because they use a lot of foreign words and the pictures are just of old weather-beaten statues, but still it's *The Indian Book of Love*, you know?

So anyway, when the five days were up, we decided to keep the book because we figured if they ever tried to arrest us for not paying, our parents would have *them* arrested for selling a dirty book to minors. But do you think it's all right for us to keep on reading it? I mean, it won't turn us into sex maniacs or anything will it? it won't give us warts or make black hair grow out of our noses?

ROCKWELL: *It may be the weather, of course, this Bermuda low. Ah, here comes a . . . .*

GIRL 3: Well, I . . . Of course, I like all the books we read for class. This wasn't for class? . . . . Oh. Well, what did the other kids say? Do you know if Sally Cameron liked it? She's the most popular girl in our class. If she likes something, I usually like it, too. . . . Oh. Well, have you read it? . . . . Oh. Well, could you come to my house later and ask me? If my mother isn't home, I could run next door and get . . . . Oh yes, I read it. I read it twice. I thought we were going to have class discussion on it. . . . . Well, it's a nice *long* book, but it's not *too* long. Don't you think some books are . . .

(*tape mutilated*)

ROCKWELL: *A small, pale rat-like boy is running toward me, shaking his fist!*

BOY 5 (shouting): My-father-says-it's-against - the - law - to - send - that - kind - of - book - to - someone - my - age - Nakedness - Toilet paper - Underwear - Love - He - said - to - call - the - police - if - anyone - tried - to - talk - to - me - about - it - POLICE!   POLICE!   POL

BOY 6: What's George yelling for the police for?

BOY 7: Hey, George! Why're you yelling?

POLICE! POLICE! POLICE!

BOY 6: *Him*? What'd he *do*, George? *The Portmanteau Book*? No kidding? Geez, I read some of it the night our TV busted. It didn't seem like much to me. I mean, *Bugs Bunny* is sexier. What'd you think, Bill?

BOY 7: *I* didn't read it.

POLICE! POLICE! POLICE!

BOY 6: D'you read it, Sally?

GIRL 4: I thought it was stupid. I mean, who wants to read a story about a *duck*? And the comic was just silly. It . . .

ROCKWELL: *Didn't you like the Cookbook?*

POLICE! POLICE! POLICE!

GIRL 4: That's even *stupider*. That's so stupid I thought my brother Albert had written it. Boy, is that a *stupid, stupid* book.

BOY 7: Yeah. I'll bet if you saw the author, he'd look like this:

ROCKWELL: *Did it ever occur to any of you that you might be the ones who are stupid, not the author? that . . .*

POLICE! POLICE! POLICE! POLICE! POLICE! POL

BOY 7: *Who's* stupid?

GIRL 4: *Me*? *I'm* stupid? You're calling *me* stupid?

BOY 6: Hey. What's he getting so mad about anyway?

BOY 7: Yeah, what's it to you, Mister? You didn't write the book. You're just an interviewer.

POLICE! HERE HE IS, OFFICER! THIS IS HIM! ARREST HIM! ARREST HIM! HE'S THE

(*Static, bleeps, thumps, doors slamming, sirens*)

ROCKWELL (subdued, hoarse, desperate): *Summary so far — reactions to* THE PORTMANTEAU BOOK *were mixed. It was preferred to fried eggplant but not to carrots, beans, peas, and corn. Liver and salmon loaf were not mentioned. Bail was set at $200.*

(END OF TAPE)

The End . . .